A CRISIS OF SAINTS

GEORGE WILLIAM RUTLER

A CRISIS OF SAINTS

Essays on People and Principles
"The real danger to society is
not merely a lack of virtue
but a lack of heroism."

IGNATIUS PRESS   SAN FRANCISCO

Cover art: Annibale Carracci
Christ Appearing to Saint Peter on the Appian Way,
"Domine Quo Vadis", National Gallery, London
Bridgeman/Art Resource, NY

Cover design by Roxanne Mei Lum

Haud ignara mali miseris succurrere disco

Aeneid I. 630

CONTENTS

PREFACE

It had been my intention to call this book *Insensitive Essays,* to preempt any critic accustomed to such language who might call them that. It would have been a fair description, in any event, because the essays do not have as their chief purpose, or as a purpose at all, the cultivation of notions of ease in an uncomfortable time and satisfaction in a restless time. Then I thought I might qualify the title by calling the book *Insensitive Essays for Insensitive People,* but that would prejudice the case against the readers, all of whom probably have been called more pointed things by sensitive people. Or I might have called it *Insensitive Essays for Sensitive People,* but that would suggest I had about me the spirit of the curmudgeon, a figure of social benefit in these days of malignant sentimentality, but one which might promote a spirit contrary to the Christian profession.

So I chose the title which is as much a theme as any for these essays, which are written far past the twilight of a century of mixed expectations and accomplishments. A mystical anticipation about the year 2000 is brooding already, and we shall have to wait to see whether it is of a nature different from the attentions at the end of the first Christian millennium. If we go by the credible opinions of historians, 1994 may have been the two thousandth anniversary of the Incarnation. If that is so, and if it passed with little notice, it was not unlike the Incarnation itself. The events of Christ are not to be kept as anniversaries anyway. They are far more than occasions. They are the motive of history, and to keep the Incarnation merely as a birthday could be like making the Mass a testimonial dinner. The force of the Incarnation gains momentum as each year moves toward the consummation of all time. The first thing

that counts from the human point of view is the human participation in the unfolding events.

All I really have to say about this is that each turning point in
history is a test of holiness, and the saints make the big difference in the world's fortunes. As a corollary to this, since holiness is marked by heroic virtue, the real danger to society is not
merely a lack of virtue but a lack of heroism. Moral weakness
has been the bane of this century's last years, and it has been not
less so in the life of the Church. I would simply analyze how
this is so, either by example or implication, from the experience
of past figures and their relation to the present situation. This
may contradict certain expectations dear to well-intentioned
people of fixed habits. But where their expectations have failed,
the evidence is clear and needs only illustration. A century
from now that will be easier to do, but we have to begin where
we are, and that first of all means stopping the denial of the way
things are. T. S. Eliot said with coruscating simplicity, in *Burnt
Norton:* "Human kind / Cannot bear very much reality." But if
we would consummate our lives in the Really Real, our beginning has to be in the recognition of reality.

Chapter Six draws on the substance of remarks I made at a
symposium of the Wethersfield Institute held at Columbia University. I am grateful to the Homeland Foundation for allowing
me to include material from my contribution at this meeting.
Chapter Seven enlarges my introduction to *More Quotable
Chesterton,* published by Ignatius Press.

I

THE WORST AND BEST OF TIMES

The Guise of Reform

When Pope Pius IV died on the ninth of December in 1565, neither Rome nor the world around Rome looked very promising. Even the glitter of the New World was beginning to tarnish, for beyond the waved ocean lay many of the same problems of the old lands besides new human and material burdens. As a malaise, the situation has some familiar ring in these years after the enthusiasms of man's walk on the moon. An increasing cynicism about new things and achievements has promoted indifference to excellence and invention under the guise of cultural pluralism; the term New World has become suspect, and the past generation's romance about space exploration has degenerated into nature mysticism and an obsession with the extinction of Planet Earth. As for pluralism, the philosophers of indifferentism would be scandalized by Saul Bellow's very sensible question: "Where is the Tolstoy of the Zulus? The Proust of the Papuans? I'd be glad to read him." In 1565, the temptation to a cultural and moral depression similar to ours was not so ideological or stupid. A new maturity about the new lands was the more positive gift of discovery, and man was beginning to learn that there is a difference between exploration and running away from home and that there is no hope for society or the soul that does not begin at home. It is a lesson we are being taught by the distress of our native culture. It was that way more than four centuries ago, too, and has always been so. If the late Renaissance world was reassessing its hopefulness about the new age abroad, its domestic analysis was also sobering.

In the dying days of Pius IV, the condition of the European homeland hurt even more than the new colonies, for civilization hung in the balance with the Turk menacing Hungary and, if Hungary, then all Europe. The next year, the Turks would actually dare to lay siege to Szigetvár as only the beginning of raucous threats. Fortifying Rome and funding the war with Islam cost the papal coffers hundreds of thousands of scudi; there was little left to rehabilitate the Papal States and to finance reforms in the Church. And for reform the Church's better angels cried, for Islam was from without, but heresy was from within, and the ecumenical council that had closed two years earlier had barely begun to be understood. The previous year, Protestantism had been restored to England and was spreading through Germany and Austria and the Lowlands; 1562 had seen a Dutch conspiracy to drive Cardinal Granvelle from power and Calvinism had secured the freedom of its own French cities. Under Luther's guise of reform and renewal, an entire ecclesiastical revision was under way, and the confusion he caused was made noisier by Melancthon and Calvin, who claimed that what they were doing was Catholic while what they were destroying was not Catholic but "Papist". They had sympathizers in Rome and among the bishops and were artful in exploiting the new medium of the press, though the proliferation of primers and catechetical books disproves an old propaganda that Catholics were wanting in their use of printing or that they actually opposed it.

The majority of bishops meant to be faithful, but many lacked the theological equipment for their work. They were, by nature and formation, passive in their works. Until the Council of Trent first met in 1545 to spell out the case, the leaders of the Church tended to silence, intimidated in part by the increasing enthusiasm of scholars for the slogan "evangelical freedom", which in application could easily be made to mean philosophical independence. The catch phrase also became a convenient piety for priests who wanted to break their vows. In the face of such chaos, the shocked reaction of ordinary Catholics might lead to dismay or resignation, but there were hierarchs who chose the form of denial. This seemed prudent, but it was of the lowest spiritual order. It did not deny the world in the holy sense, it only denied what was going on in the world. The late historian Hubert Jedin described the state of things back then from a poignant modern perspective in his famous memorandum of 1968: "The schism of the Church succeeded by nothing so much as by the illusion that it did not exist."

A tendency to unreality, or psychological denial, is the poison of any culture that has calculated its agenda apart from the intense realism typical of saints. The poison has an antidote, however bitter it may taste to the lethargic. It has three ingredients. Saint Francis de Sales wrote of them, but the benign alchemy was summed up before him by Louis of Granada. These are regular prayer (neglect of which destroys the taste for things of God); contempt for inordinate self-love (which prevents loss of the right perspective on the self and everything outside the self); and cultivation of those virtues proper to one's state in life (lest the devil of distraction dissipate energy).

The soul needs these to deal with the vast historic panorama that underlies any smaller concern of culture. The encyclical *Veritatis Splendor* calls it "the final and unutterable mystery from which we take our origin and toward which we tend". The daunting amount of information at the disposal of our new electronic culture seems, if anything, to have tried a detour around this mystery by uttering itself away from the unutterable. Churchmen themselves have not been innocent of wordiness, not uncommonly hacking away at unreadable and unread pastoral letters. But the mystery cannot be gotten around, it can only be ignored. Massive information has become an avenue to massive ignorance. This is expressed through relativism, or the notion that the final and unutterable mystery is neither final nor unutterable but is rather an attitude of the moment which anyone is free to express. The deepest mystery of life's meaning has become just a puzzle about why we are alive, and in that jumbled puzzle there is no truth other than the freedom to try to escape the truth. Easy then it is to be like Mr. Batts in Newman's novel *Loss and Gain,* which was published in a year, 1848, possibly comparable to 1989 for its revolutionary impact on European social theory: his "British and Foreign Truth Society" maintained (under the patronage of Cicero, Peter Abelard and Benjamin Franklin) that "(1) It is uncertain whether Truth exists. (2) It is certain that it cannot be found." Uncertain certitude so lush as this makes man a puzzle to himself and creates the cracks for a general cultural breakdown: not so much a nervous breakdown as a philosophical breakdown. Doing my own thing takes precedence over doing the right thing. And since any lie can be arrived at logically if you begin with a lie, the lie that I have the autonomous right to do my own thing regardless of what is right ends up meaning that nothing is right apart from the "rightness" I give it. Such is the mental diction of those who say with a tone of profundity, "That may be right for you, but it's not right for me." Ten years before addressing this sentimental separation of the freedom to act from responsibility to reality, John Paul II warned some Jesuit educators about a relativism "which leads to an unfounded primacy of freedom over truth, practice over theory, becoming over being". Here is the psychology behind the substitution of value for virtue and the pursuit of "values clarification" instead of virtuousness.

Paradox radiates in this: one becomes more and more free the more one obeys the truth. This is truth's "splendor"; it is splendid in itself for being true and splendid for our souls by setting us free from unreality. Cardinal Newman was too charitable and sensitive to speak violently of his philosophical opponents; the most indicting thing he called them from time to time was "unreal", and that word on the lips of so real a man was palpably withering. Relativism is the attempt to realize unreality. It defies the Incarnation of Christ. For while "the Word was made flesh and dwelt among us", the relativist's creed chants: "the Impression was made flesh and dwelt within us." It is not thinking at all; it is feeling without thinking.

A Logic of the Soul

Now, feeling without thinking creates an enormous sentimen-
talist prejudice, and the first perceptible evidence of sentimentalism is, curiously enough, ugliness. Beauty consists in a thing
being ordered according to its rightful purpose, but when
truth is denied, purpose is obscured, and that obscurity of
purpose, and not visual appearance, is the ground of philosophical ugliness. Beauty, and ugliness, then, cannot be properly
understood in the line of feeling detached from reason. Feeling
is right and good only when it accords with truth; the affective
is obliged to the effective. In solid Aristotelian tradition, Aquinas
attached the psychological characteristic of beauty's ability to
please the senses to a philosophical condition that it have integrity,
right proportion and clarity. Aesthetics, properly, is then concerned with virtue; and the attempt to create beauty without
virtue is vain aestheticism. One measure of a man's virtue is the
sort of things that give him pleasure. Every decadent culture
has withered into a perfumed and passive aestheticism that way,
and the emphasis invariably is on pleasure and appearance
detached from sacrifice and honesty. No one should be surprised,
then, if the decadent culture is characterized by a crisis of
identity and a simultaneous preoccupation with human respect
and luxury. In the life of the Church, this takes the form of
denuding worship and ritual for the sake of personal comfort
and self-indulgence; and party to this is the luxurious tendency
to accommodate and even sanction liturgical abuses for the sake
of a superficial institutional unity. We are created to worship
God, through whom we find our meaning; and if we do not
worship "in spirit and truth", it will be impossible to define the
Church, the priest, the world, the family and the self. The fruit
of the Spirit is "love, joy, peace, patience, kindness, goodness,
faithfulness, gentleness, self-control; against these there is no
law" (Gal 5:22–23).

I mention this not as a digression, for it helps to explain the
various sloughs of the spirit through which the Church Mili-

tant has passed and is passing now. As it was in the sixteenth century, so is it now, only now it is amplified by larger populations. Reform now, as always, will come about by addressing the meaning and purpose of the human being. The worst times in human history have been caused by neglect of these realities; the best times have been the work of people humble enough to be shocked into the truth by the ugliness of such neglect. It can never be said enough: any crisis in culture is a crisis of saints, and no reform is radical enough unless it is a redemption from sin.

Shortly before the publication of *Veritatis Splendor,* the wife of a very highly placed public official declared in a speech that if America is to be reformed, it will need a new definition of human beings for the twenty-first century. She spoke with breathless sincerity and an aura of humanity; she even went to Texas to do it, and she gave reality a black eye. Logic was unharmed by her conclusion only if it began with the lie that there is no human soul. For the human soul is a life-giving spirit, the "form" of the body that defines human being. Because earthly life is fleeting, the Samoans call the soul "that which comes and goes". But the fact of the soul is not fleeting, and I can understand the significance of its coming and going only if I do not pretend to have the authority to make it come and go.

The soul is not rightly understood if it is the "idea" of the body: that was the notion of those philosophers, the Cartesians, who radically separated soul and body. Political Cartesians speak glibly about separating Church and State, as though spiritual and social realities can be segregated without violating reality. Eventually, then, morality must become schizophrenia, and the loudest social reformers will maintain that moral acts are like any matters of personal taste. But the human soul is the "form" of the body in the sense that it makes man conscious of himself in relation to past, present and future. The souls of animals endow biological life but not spiritual life: thus animals have no analytical history or imagination. Animals make sounds to communicate certain behavioral instincts, but they could never say "was" or "will be", because they cannot say "I". If my perception of "me" denies God, who is my source, my self-consciousness bewilders myself. Ask Adam and Eve. And the way to ask them is to ask anyone who says we must redefine human beings. For all its posturing, that call for redefinition is a shout of bravado cloaking the embarrassment of having become a question mark. But man must be a puzzle if he has cancelled out the divine mystery. That he does when he tries to resolve it on his own terms. Either he defines himself as an animal, as have done the modern materialists, or as a phantasm, as have done the superstitious clients of New Age theosophy. Now theosophy is half theology and half philosophy, theology without God and philosophy without wisdom, which means it thinks God is the self and the self is God. When you are half-right about divinity and humanity, you are totally wrong about both. For in this, at least, theology and philosophy are like baseball: you are not safe if you do not quite touch base.

To the subjectivist, the power to define is tantamount to the power to create. The definition becomes "virtual reality", which is quite why the existentialist Jean-Paul Sartre could say with a straight face, "Man creates his own essence." This was the boast of existentialism, and it was to existence what racism is to race. Sartre had not passed part of his existence in Auschwitz, which had been built by a state philosophy intent on creating its own essence. Viktor Frankl, one of psychiatry's healthier pioneers, had been within its spiked fences and had smelled its smoke, and yet his reply to Sartre was politely measured: "I don't think man creates his own essence. I rather think he detects it." Detection of essence is growth in wisdom, and wisdom does not seek to redefine for any century what has been defined for all centuries: God created man in his own image and likeness.

Uncontrolled Freedom

That encyclical on the splendor of truth appeared in the same season in which we heard the politician's wife appeal for a new definition of us for the next century. In it the Pope summoned understatement: "Certain tendencies in contemporary moral theology, under the influence of subjectivism and individualism, . . . involve novel interpretations of . . . human nature. . . . " The remark sounds almost off-handed, but its meaning is from the right hand of God. Redefinition of the self, that primordial lie that constructed the original sin, divorces freedom from truth so totally that human history since then has been an unrelieved moral slavery. The Pope says clearly that freedom uncontrolled by truth leads to tyranny. The ego becomes the constant tyrant, but the ego can project itself into whole cultures and political movements; any tyranny, be it that of a dictator or that of a muddled philosophical climate, is the replacement of God by the ego writ large.

In the nineteenth century, Émile Zola wrote a novel based on an authenticated miraculous cure of Marie Lebranchu at Lourdes, which he had witnessed on August 20, 1890. He refused to acknowledge that a miracle could happen, so his novel described the cure as psychosomatic, and the character La Grivotte, who was based on the woman in fact, soon died, as the woman in fact did not. A certain Dr. Boissarie asked him how he could be so free with the facts, so unscientific, and Zola replied: "My characters belong to me. I have the right to do with them as I will. I can make them live or die as it pleases me." For the subjectivist, life is a novel, and the self is the novelist. *"Mes personnages m'appartiennent. . . . "* It is the metaphysical myth of the so-called Age of Science, and it is as unscientific as it thinks itself scientific. The subjectivist is prejudiced, and ultimately he is prejudiced by the most tyrannical power, the "I" uncontrolled by the "Thou" which is objective truth personified. In his arbitrary prejudice, he is anxious to expose the Church's crimes against science, and he has made a pseudoscience of this prejudice so subtly that, like Zola, he cannot see his bias. He still does not apologize, for example, at refusing to accept the Gregorian reform of the Julian calendar simply because a pope was the reformer. Not until 1752 did England and the Protestant world accept the more mathematically precise calendar of Gregory XIII, with its reckoning of leap year, which most of the Catholic world started to use in 1578. Even when it was accepted, there were demonstrations in the streets of London by people who thought the Romish system of astronomy was taking eleven days out of their lives.

My creatures belong to me! Reality is what I define reality to be. Transcendent contradiction of human willfulness has to be mocked into submission. The contemporary criticism of the Church for being obscurantist and an obstacle to progress is but one slightly more sophisticated version of an old diatribe. Thus in 1936 a sign appeared on a bulletin board of the Hitler Youth headquarters at Halle on the Saale: "Where are the enemies of our Hitler youth? They are the religious fanatics who still today fall on their knees with wistful looks directed upward, who spend their time attending churches and praying. We, as Hitler boys, can regard only with contempt or derision young people who still today run to their ridiculous Evangelical or Catholic clubs to give themselves up to eminently superfluous religious reveries." So there is nothing new about the cry for a new definition of human beings, except that now it is made in the name of the twenty-first century. But it is what the National Socialists wanted for the twentieth century and the Economic Socialists for the nineteenth and the Deist Socialists for the eighteenth. The social contribution of each was to self-destruct. Biological Socialists want to do the defining now, and their self-destruction is the inevitable prediction of their own thesis. Biological Socialists are those who would use the institutions of government and education and the arts to propagate eugenics through scientific technology independent of obedience to natural law. In this matrix of the social engineers, life is an option rather than a right. The original temptation along these lines was at the start of the human adventure, in the temptation to eat of the tree of the knowledge of good and evil. This was not the denial to humans of information. To eat of the tree meant that the man and the woman could redefine what was good and evil for them apart from what is good and evil. The fruit was illusion, and the consequent loss of Paradise was a loss of authentic perception. And all this because the Voice of Contradiction proposed to Man and Woman that they redefine themselves: not Man and Woman. Gods! And so they did. As did Zola and each of us in our weak moments, which at the time we think are our strong moments. And when the true God walked their way in the cool of the evening, they hid behind a real tree wrapped only in their false definition. They shivered, and because we still have a derivative of the preternatural intelligence they lost, a thing called conscience, we call that shivering "shame".

All of the philosophical fig leaves of the modern experience could not cover the misuse of reason. The result, sad to say, was not something so harmless as an abstract idea; abstractions can have monstrous social incarnations; and if that were not so, the Book of Revelation was a dour exercise in pessimism, and the twisted events of the twentieth century were forgettable vignettes, and Pollyanna was a prophet. There was, however, something really prophetic in a well-known etching from Goya's *Caprichos* series, showing a man asleep at his desk, surrounded by nightmarish figures of cats and bats and owls, and inscribed "El sueño de la razón produce monstruos." Aldous Huxley, probably correctly, was not satisfied to settle for a rationalist interpretation meaning that monsters issue from the sleep of reason; it more likely illustrates, as in the iconic example of the French Reign of Terror, that monsters spring up when reason dreams on its own of utopias of technology and anthropological adventures of inevitable progress.

The Real Pentecost

In any age, people have been rudely awakened from the night-mare of reason as a religion of itself, and when their eyes have opened they have reflected on the mistakes of the human race. There is nothing new in doing so. But there is a heavier obligation to do so at the end of the twentieth century, because we have so much more evidence to cite. Evidently, this has not made us wiser, though it may make us more cynical or indifferent. That, I am afraid, would only serve to take us back to the noblest, but also most pagan, of the Greeks, whose elegant social critics looked with disdain upon the moral rot around them. Thucydides describes the gradual and constant lowering of moral standards after the Peloponnesian War, but, as much as it grieves him, there is a certain *hauteur* that says, "What more can you expect from people?" But with a Christian saint like Basil, writing about as many years after the Incarnation as Thucydides wrote before it, the tone is all different, with a passion that the first Greek critical historian would have considered in questionable taste. Basil laments to the bishops of Italy and Gaul during the Arian crisis:

> The accurate observance of the canons is no more; there is no restraint upon sin. Unbelievers laugh at what they see, and the weak are unsettled; faith is doubtful, ignorance is poured over their souls, because the adulterators of the word in wickedness imitate the truth. Religious people keep silence, but every blaspheming tongue is let loose. Sacred things are profaned; those of the laity who are sound in faith avoid the places of worship, as schools of impiety, and raise their hands in solitude with groans and tears to the Lord in Heaven.

The old Greek got his stately detachment from his confidence in Fate; the saint breathed outrage at offended Providence. The clients of Olympus showed respect for their gods by unruffled rectitude; but a louder bellow comes from the saints of the

Incarnate One who tossed men out of the Temple along with their trash.

This modern age has been a cataract of crises on a scale that would have stunned any veteran of classical wars and Arian onslaughts, and perhaps only the remove of several generations or even centuries will allow a clear appreciation of their significance. Some recent events that seemed critical, along with their heroes and villains, will be forgotten, while future critics will be amazed at how many significant events were overlooked in our time. It is an historical habit: the Passion of Christ had little public notice. That having been said, we have little excuse for ignoring what is happening. The Church is sorely afflicted in obvious ways, and only the grossest unreality can deny this. The weakness of many who should be right guides is breathtakingly apparent in this moment, and the much-publicized contempt for authority is at least matched by failure to exercise authority. Should a great reformer happen on the scene, he will be severely crippled by the lassitude of the present.

Perhaps the representative case of our age was the publication of the encyclical *Humanae Vitae* in 1968. It was an example of the grace of state at work, for Paul VI, as Pope, was prevented by the Holy Spirit from teaching other. This is not to say that the human factor was irrelevant; the Pope showed personal courage in choosing to publish it when he did. Nevertheless, the human element was very human. It may be argued that in the human order no authentic papal teaching was so badly implemented: from the advertising of an ambiguously qualified advisory committee and the confusion about its authoritative nature from the day of its release to the astonishing fact that the Holy Father did not mention it again for ten years. Indeed, he issued no encyclicals after it and shrank from indicated disciplines in its behalf. His consequent suffering was the price of his own sensitivity up against a senseless and unmannerly culture and surely earned him much merit. But history will not be able to overlook the human shortcomings. As Newman said of moral law in the first of his lectures of 1850 on *Certain Difficulties Felt by Anglicans in Catholic Teaching:* "Moralists lay down, that a law loses its authority which the lawgiver knowingly allows to be infringed and put aside...."

Newman's prestige is not to be gainsaid, and it may be said that he is already, informally at least, a Doctor of the Church, as he enjoys the unique distinction of being the one recent voice quoted as an authority in the new Catechism and the encyclical *Veritatis Splendor.* For a reference chiseled even more deeply in the foundations of the Church's thought, the Angelic Doctor writes of the legitimate use of authority: "Men who are well disposed are led to virtue by being admonished better than by coercion, but men who are evilly disposed are not led to virtue unless they are coerced" (S. Th. III, q. 94, a. 1). The Gospel message is a matter of life and death, in orders spiritual and social, but its persuasiveness is hindered by the scandal of disorder within the local churches and curias. "For if a man does not know how to manage his own household, how can he care for God's church?" (1 Tim 3:5). It may be argued that our problems have their match in past moments. It may be more cogently argued that our experience of crises is harsher because of the manifest unwillingness to confront them at the expense of the idol of the day, public image and the rapidity with which the contagion of error spreads by global communications.

I hope this gives license in charity to introduce the theme of anything significant that may follow in these pages, and if I repeat it too often, I only mean to make the case clearer: in the annals of all cultures, and most crucially in the course of the Church on earth, vice has been vicious as its nature, but weakness has done more harm than vice. There have been, as prominent examples, popes who failed in the private estate of their souls but who secured the greater good of many; and there have been goodly and even saintly popes whose lack of regimen impeded the common good of the Church. In the shadowy times of the tenth century, John XII was rapacious in every way, and no less were those who let this eighteen-year-old take the Chair of Peter; but his scarlet life whitened much outside it, as he reformed bureaucracy, encouraged Spain under the Muslim yoke, reformed monastic life and promoted a saint, Dunstan, to Canterbury. The refractory temperament of Julius II did not fracture the Faith of the Church; and Alexander VI rose from his notorious nest to promote orthodoxy, regulate the Religious houses and send confessors to the New World. Yet by contrast, a virtuous Adrian II, willing to sacrifice domestic pleasures provided him by the customs of the ninth century, failed to bring security spiritual or temporal to the Carolingian lands and watched Bulgaria slide from the Church. In the thirteenth century, Celestine V prayed in a way that has him now on the calendar of saints, but his election was a preposterous mockery of his incompetence, and he died near Ferentino in unprecedented retirement from the papacy, having practically mortgaged the College of Cardinals to the Anjou kings. The unworldly and pious Benedict XIII set out to reform clerical morals in the space of half a dozen years, and by his death in 1730 he had only managed to mismanage the Papal States into bankruptcy. If harmless in private morals, Clement XIV devastated world civilization by his untimely suppression of the Jesuits, and mankind still reels from his surrender to mere kings. None of this contradicts the principle that crises of culture are crises of saints; it does mean, however, that great saints must have minds as strong as hearts, and backbones strong as both.

The lesson is painful but crucial for our time, which has been marked by reluctance of leadership. The solution has to be in the wisdom of the Church which has made leadership a three-fold economy of prophet, priest and king. While in many ways we live in a golden age of prophecy, and when priestliness has withstood diabolic assault, the voice of the king is wanted. When the Church speaks of shepherds to lead the flock, she speaks of shepherd kings. It is a grave mistake to think that love thrives outside order or that the "pastoral" approach must be nondirective. An important address was made by the 1967

Synod of Bishops to dissenters from the Church's teaching: those "who are rash or imprudent should be warned in all charity", and after that "those who are pertinacious should be removed from office." That was solid apostolic stuff; but it became a lesser thing, I am in no position to call it weak tea, when the extraordinary Synod of 1985 revised the advice and said only that "communication and reciprocal dialogue between bishops and theologians are necessary for the building up of faith and its deeper comprehension."

The present state of pastoral *ennui* in the Church, dangerously courting paganism in its cynicism and mistaken in its tendency to treat solicitude and discipline as opposites, is no more daunting than the sense of disappointment in those who had expected their generation to reverse decay. Refusal to exercise legitimate authority when prudence wants it can be pride dressed as humility. Ambitious words have been spoken, inflated by immense and expensive bureaucratic programs in the affluent West unshamed by the countless twentieth-century martyrs in other parts of the world. In the sound of their own echoes, they have already become vacuous and innocent of action. But this is the nature of bureaucracy, which, de Tocqueville said in the second volume of *Democracy in America,* "does not break men's will, but softens, bends, and guides it; it seldom enjoins, but often inhibits, action; it does not destroy anything, but prevents much being born. . . . " Classical economies of the virtues have been unanimous: prudence is a virtue as prelude to an action, and not as a substitute for it.

Saint Thomas More was martyr to this meanness of the human spirit and appealed with holy exasperation to the bishops of his moment. From the Tower he wrote in his *De Tristitia Christi* (Of the Sadness of Christ): "[The bishop] hides away cowering in some cranny, and abandons the ship to the waves. If a bishop does this, I would not hesitate to juxtapose and compare his sadness with the sadness that leads . . . to hell." The one bishop of that time who made Christ happy with his bravery, Saint John Fisher, warned his fellow apostles: "The

fort is betrayed even by them that should have defended it."
Looking about him as the scaffold loomed, he mourned on
behalf of the others who would not mourn: "Everything is
turned upside down, the beautiful order of virtue was over-
thrown, the bright light of life quenched, and scarce anything
left in the church but open iniquity and feigned sanctity . . .
innumerable souls are falling into destruction."

Ours was to have been a time of renewal in the Church, but
sometimes it seems to have been a baptism of tentative virtue
and a confirmation of the fatuities of the Aquarian Age. Clerics
of the 1960s who had not seen real flames talked of a New
Pentecost which has not come. Some in their greying years
keep scanning some horizon beyond the horizon and persist in
speaking of the Second Vatican Council as The Council. As
they age, they ache when they are called naïve. But naïve they
have been. It was perhaps in view of this that the late Cardinal
Siri of Genoa said that it would take centuries to undo the
damage after Vatican II. He paid a price for saying that, exacted
by banal optimists who would have confused the Holy Spirit
with UNICEF or Eleanor Roosevelt. Siri did not challenge the
authenticity of the Council, but he rejected a conciliar tri-
umphalism which in its romance saw nothing blasphemous in
treating Vatican II as if it were Pentecost II.

There is no need for the Holy Spirit to come back to the
Church. He has never left the Church. Legitimate renewal
consists in recognizing his presence and obeying it. Illegitimate
renewal, however, would speak of entering an entirely new
anthropological stage. This was the mistake of many, though
happily not all, theologians at the time of Vatican II. It may
explain why the general tone of that Council, for all its expressions which the Holy Spirit protected from error, in some ways
misread the course of world events as they were about to
unfold. The assumption seemed to be that official state secularism had no self-destructive logic. Economic dialecticism was
avoided gingerly as a power that would be around for a long
time; and so was lost a momentous chance to prophesy the

inevitable collapse — by supernatural promise and agency — of a truly evil empire. Nor was there any expressed anticipation of pastoral confusion in the Church's liturgical and moral life. Even the self-conscious progressivist Edward Schillebeeckx, who has lately so clearly distanced himself from the Magisterium, expressed surprise in the early 1970s in *The Mission of the Church* at how the "almost naïve" enthusiasms of Vatican II for developments in scientific technology gave such short shrift to the aesthetical importance of arts and letters.

While one may still hope for a realization of the best expressions of Vatican II, and while fanatical disparagements of the Council's legitimacy must be deplored as offensive to the guarantees of the Holy Spirit, perhaps only Lateran V was as unsuccessful in solving the problems it addressed. It took Trent to reform the Lateran reform, and in the same order authentic reform may come only through a generation for whom Vatican II is understood as a council and not The Council. Those disposed to think in terms of The Council tend to think of the Church as postconciliar. The gentle intoxication of that expression is only gradually being discovered, and its lack of historical perspective will soon cease to be an endearing little way of aging scholars and will become an embarrassment. There is no such thing as a postconciliar Church. The Church of Vatican II is the Church of Nicaea and all other councils. There will be, however, postconciliar generations, and they may not think of themselves as postconciliar at all, for they may have their own councils. That will happen when easy confidences about the future mature into a more reasonable analysis of history and the development of doctrine. Such sobriety mingled with virtue is the stuff of saints.

And, by way of corollary, this recovery of spiritual sanity will have humor as one of its signs. For humor is among other things the perception of imbalance as imbalanced and the appreciation of incongruity as incongruous. Self-absorbed observers are not observers at all, and so they tend to humorlessness; they lack a platform in reality from which to measure the lack of measure around them. In the present life of culture, and certainly in this moment of the Church, extremists on the left and on the right have a common inability to laugh at themselves. Healthy jokes are to them like a strange sound frequency to a dog: they turn their heads, they look distressed, but they do not laugh. The years after Vatican II, which were supposed to bring fresh air to the Church, did not bring fresh laughter. We do not expect humor in encyclicals; but incidental works of apologetics are unwell when humor is totally absent. Something is very wrong when the only humor in diocesan newspapers is unintentional. What is worst about the manners of our times is the awkwardness of attempts at humor that laugh at things balanced and congruous. As this takes its course, laughter will not be the only lost gift: there will be no gift of tears in the confessionals and no gift of singing at the altars. And all because we took seriously the most incongruous notion that we had finally balanced the world. From such an implausible view of life, the only thing that makes people laugh is cruelty: cruelty to the beautiful, cruelty to the truthful, cruelty to the good.

Ichabod

Recall the bleakness of that day Pope Pius IV died. The Pope had been a gigantic figure in the political forum from a long experience of dealing with hostile parties, pragmatic in reforms and sophisticated in the cultural obligations of the Church, as his universities, presses and civic monuments attest. The ordering of his own household and government was more fragile, and, although he was an active initiator of the Tridentine reforms, little would have come of that great work had it not been for the steady labor of his holy nephew, Archbishop Borromeo of Milan. The brightest flower of nepotism tempered his uncle's diverse enthusiasms and brought to fruition the decrees of the Council, which, if left to the Pope's agency, would have been a torrent of words flooding the world and irrigating little. The Pope died in a Rome newly ornamented with the Porta Pia and the Villa Pia in his own gardens and the Baths of Diocletian renovated as a glorious shrine to Mary of the Angels, but disappointment in him was obvious to the length that his life had been threatened by his own people. Yet when his scarred and ambitious journey ended, it was his happiness that three saints attended the papal deathbed: Philip Neri, who converted the soul of the Rome which the Pope had only refurbished; Charles Borromeo, who rose through a corrupt system to change it; and Michele Ghislieri, who as Pius V would make the theory of holiness a fact from Mexico to Africa and India.

Each of these men was decidedly different in character and wit, but they were focused and were not partymen to compromise. They needed no prodding in doing what had to be done to incarnate theory. Pius V strained unsuccessfully to match his predecessor's diplomatic skills; diplomat he was not, but his fleet at Lepanto helped to save Christian civilization, and that is a fact. All of them prayed the Mass, not in a new way, but in the old way renewed, knowing that the dignity of man is marked by the dignity he gives God at the altar. In this there was no compromise, no vacillating and no cynical condescension. Authentic renewal is of the saints, and it is hymned in their polyphony played against our guitars. The recent anguish in the Church's liturgical experience is of a sadder order. Sanctuaries are chaotic, and the response tends to bewilderment, then denial, then surrender. Bureaucratic resolve to move liturgical abuses past toleration to sanction, as in the clericalization of the laity in roles of service in the sanctuary, shows how elements of renewal can become machines of dissolution. And when, for example, permission was given for local churches to delete portions of the fifth chapter of the Letter to the Ephesians and the third chapter of the Letter to the Colossians if those local churches think the offending passages are antifeminist, we saw how far the prophetic office of the Church had been compromised in its duty to stretch the human mind to the heights of God. Not everyone who resents this is a crank, and not everyone who laments this is a reactionary in the bad sense. Only utopian progressivism thinks that all reaction is wrong. Only the dead fail to react. Telling bad news about fallen man can be obedience to the Good News about man redeemed. Nor are they necessarily negative who point out that not everything is positive.

The situation finds prophetic voice in the ancient bereavement of the Jews. When the Philistines had conquered the Israelites, the wife of Phinehas gave birth to a son whom she named Ichabod, a mourning name meaning "the glory has departed." Her father-in-law, Eli, had collapsed and died at the capture of the Ark of the Covenant, and Phinehas, with his brother Hophni, had been killed in its defense. The woman said in a spirit of utter realism transcending moroseness, "The glory has departed from Israel, for the ark of God has been captured" (1 Sam 4:22). That was a fact, and by God's grace it did not remain so for long. When the Philistines tried to bring the Ark into their false sanctuary, the idol Dagon collapsed before it. For a sad while, however, Israel was bereft, and civilizations have learned from such grief. The name of that sense of loss has become a literary icon: in nineteenth-century America, Daniel Webster was called Ichabod in poetry when his compromise on slavery bitterly disappointed those for whom he had been a promised liberator.

To meanderers on the Emmaus road, Ichabod seemed written on the sunset sky. They knew only the death of Christ, not that he had risen. The glory in fact had never left, save in human perception. That does not make the sense of loss less like Calvary or any twilight. The early chapters of the Book of Revelation record the voice of the glorified Christ telling the early churches of Asia Minor the way things really are. Their Christians failed when they were transformed by their culture, and they prevailed when they transformed their culture. In the history of the universal Church, the victory of the cross is secure, but any particular church can fail if it succumbs to unreality about the human condition. The Church is guaranteed until the end of time, but the local churches of Asia Minor and North Africa had no local guarantee, nor does any local church, and the church in the United States or any other place can measure its integrity at least in part by the degree to which it realizes that. But we have engaged a deep denial of the spiritual crisis, and only the cold hand of current events can make wishful thinkers face the failure of ecclesiastical utopianism. The situation throughout the Church in many affluent lands is more than a parallel to the moral somnolence of the West in the face of Hitlerism. Those times, dark and horrible as they were, may be prelude to a wider spiritual crisis now facing us, a cataclysmic meeting of cultures that has already exacted unconscionable slaughters of unborn life and social decay. We are repeating, even within the Church, moral lassitude and compromises that were the bane of Britain in the 1930s, when Ramsay MacDonald (Churchill's "Boneless Wonder") preferred butter to guns because he did not estimate the kind of danger ahead, and when Neville Chamberlain thought the enemy might be held to account as a gentleman.

As we look about the Church today, at her high expectations for the moment bought at the price of prophetic witness, at her many members who have bartered her principles and Pope for a counterfeit religiosity, who invoke a tradition and spiritual ancestry only to accommodate them to their opposites, we have every right to understand how Churchill felt when he spoke in the Commons on a bleak March 24, 1938: "For five years I have talked to the House on these matters—not with very great success. I have watched this famous island descending incontinently, fecklessly, the stairway which leads to a dark gulf. It is a fine broad stairway at the beginning, but after a bit the carpet ends. A little farther on there are only flagstones, and a little farther on still these break beneath your feet...." In the particular case of our own nation, there may be slightly more than chauvinism in Clemenceau's belief that "America is the only nation in history which miraculously has gone from barbarism to degeneration without the usual interval of civilization." Mediocrity, in the Church or in civil society, lacks the capacity for rescue from the degeneracy, and groundless optimism is only a bromide for the degenerate who are starved of the bread of life.

The Church herself, however, is unique among all lesser realities in her internal means of renewal. This has been the promise made to her once for the ages by the Lord of Creation and the Redeemer of Man. These moments of renewal are the crises of saints. If there will be new centuries, there will not be a New Pentecost. While venerable voices have spoken that way in these latter days, even expecting some such thing of an ecumenical council, their language must be understood as poetic, and no more literal than calling for a New Nativity or a New Resurrection. As each Mass is an offering of the one perfect Sacrifice of Calvary and is not a New Passion, so the gifts of the Holy Spirit need not be added to; there must rather be new souls confirmed in them as history grandly cuts its gruelling way in time. Pentecost is for all time, and the time to come will be renewed by the Holy Spirit when human spirits learn to distinguish things innocent from things naïve.

II

THE GENEROSITY OF GOD

"When they got out on land, they saw a charcoal fire there, with fish lying on it, and bread. Jesus said to them, 'Bring some of the fish that you have just caught.' So Simon Peter went aboard and hauled the net ashore, full of large fish, a hundred and fifty-three of them; and although there were so many, the net was not torn" (Jn 21:10–11).

Little Children

The details in one story about Alexander of Macedon vary in the telling, but the point about his royal munificence is the same. When a beggar called out along a road, he stopped and announced that he was giving him command of several cities. The man stammered that he had only asked for a few coins, to which Alexander replied, "You ask as a beggar, I give as a king."

There is a tone of that in the resurrection appearance of the Lord on the Galilean shore. After fishing all night, seven of the disciples hear his voice calling to them to try again, casting their nets this time over the right side of the boat, and the catch is so great that the nets nearly break: they drag to shore one hundred and fifty-three large fish. This is the generosity of kings. Now, since the advent of German higher criticism in the cramped religious mentality of the nineteenth century, many Scripture scholars have approached all Bible stories as though they are suspect fishermen's tales, even the accounts of bread multiplied on land and angels appearing from air. But even some fishing tales are true. The curiosity here is that by the fishermen's own account they are not the clever ones; they are in fact passive agents at first, and the supernatural agency at work gently mocked their native skill. Fishermen not under oath do not spontaneously admit to having been helped. The logging up of the precise size of the catch shows their rattled astonishment at what had been done through them when by themselves they could do nothing.

"Little children, have you caught anything?" (Jn 21:5). Mark the "little children": *paidia*. The New English Bible muddles the text with its thumpingly flat and wrong "friends". Then it become ridiculous almost to the point of inspiration when it says the Lord, like some self-effacing servant of the Royal Yacht Squadron, "suggested" that the disciples "shoot the net starboard". The New American Bible also has our Lord speak of "starboard", compounding the nautical touch. As for the "children", even the Challoner-Rheims was no less flat when it substituted "young men". Ronald Knox tried valiantly in translation, and his Greek erudition is not to be gainsaid; but his "lads" sounds all too jolly, like a Navy chanty. The grand Authorized Version of King James has the same problem with its Englishness from time to time, as when it speaks in Exodus of Pharaoh's "butler", conjuring up a not unpleasant image of the Egyptians holding court in a stately country house before the depredations of the Labour Party. The King James, like the Revised Standard Version and the New American, renders "children", but misses the diminutive of the ordinary word for children; the point of the little children is that they are little.

There is nothing cute about this; there is nothing cute about Christ. When all else is said about Christ that humans will say before the universe shuts its doors at the end of time, no one will seriously have proposed that he was cute; they may say more problematic and even insulting things about him, but they will never presume to say that he had a trivial appeal and a merely congenial way with words. They will divide into those who think he was mad or terrible or deluded or brilliant or wonderful beyond human explanation; and when they are too desperate for any of that, they will repeat some of their ancestors' evasions by suggesting that he never existed; but not even in an asylum or university will they summarize him in that most damning phrase, "a nice man". Niceness may mean various things, but it always means that the man in question was plausible to lazy conceptions and that he preferred language harmless instead of true. If Christ never met a man he did not like, as the aphorism goes, he never told men only what they liked to hear. He comes into the world with what he has to say, and he means what he says. He had promised the men in the boat that they would no longer be called servants but friends; now there is a conscious change. Even the Jerusalem Bible misses it by still insisting against the text that he says "friends". From the fire on the shore, the Voice calls them little children as if to say that from the Paschal light all of his friends in faith are and always will be children to his glory, and helpless indeed without him. The Light of the World kindles a little fire on the shore and calls over the water solemnly and absolutely, "Little children. . . . "

This does not compromise the friendship; it literally sheds new light on it. The Father and he are one, and in the last days of his physical life on earth he participates more vividly before men in his relationship to divine paternity. As Son of the Father, he now in the name of the Father fathers his Church. His kingdom is not of this world, a point worth making exactly because his kingdom has come into this world. Any earthly effort to live without him from now on will be spectacularly childish. The full measure of human dignity begins to be recognized in this. After all, he also said once along the Palestinian roads that we cannot inherit the kingdom of heaven until we become like little children; and in their record of what he said about this kingdom, Matthew and Mark use the same "little children" that the fishermen will hear. The change of grown men into little children is of such spiritual wisdom that it is the perfect opposite of childishness.

One Hundred and Fifty-Three

Then the disciples become little children, and, as little children have sometimes done even outside parental fantasy, they do what they are told. John, who is the youngest, shouts with the exuberance of a child. Peter, who is the senior, does what older people do when they relive their youth by acting younger than the youngest; he is the first to jump into the water. And all his recently endowed Semitic dignity splashes with abandon toward the Voice. When the years have passed, they will remember these details, more with affection than with any hint of embarrassment; and one of the details, pedantic if it were not so improbable under the circumstances, will be the number of the fish. Before some modern critics took the mental shortcut of dismissing the whole event at the end of the Fourth Gospel as a coda to an illusion, great doctors of the Church believed it and considered what the number might signify.

To read meanings in a number can become a dangerous reading of meanings into a number. The Church warns against this practice, but some misguided people outside Catholic constraints have been oblivious to that caution. They persist in making a minor profession of speculating about any numbers in the sacred texts: the Apocalypse is a particularly rich mine for arcane algebra. The morose can make the number six hundred and sixty-six, for example, add up to the ages of members of the Trilateral Commission, and so on. Anyone with an adventurous right brain lobe can play that game. To a mind sufficiently elastic, the number of fish is exactly the span of years between the defeat of the Bonnie Prince at Culloden and the assassination of President McKinley; and the Battle of Tippecanoe raged one hundred and fifty-three years before the surgical removal of President Johnson's gall bladder. Given the history of religion in the United States, some new cult based on these discoveries might still spring up to take its place next to Mormonism and Seventh-Day Adventism. If even some English Methodist could be comforted by the preacher George Whitfield's way of pronouncing "that blessed word Mesopotamia", there might yet appear in Southern California a Church of the One Hundred and Fifty-Three.

All images are not imagery or of that order. When I was an undergraduate and Robert Frost used to come and read his poems, a classmate asked him the meaning of the two roads that diverged in "The Road Not Taken". He repeated the philosophical interpretations of some critics, then said that at the writing he had in his mind's eye the fork in the road south of Thetford Junction. None of us, even of us sophomores, was taken in by this coy and even somewhat morbid man; he would not have written those lines if he had only been thinking about getting around parts of Vermont; and if something had not happened at the fork, there would not be much point in talking about any other place. There is not a scrap of that disingenuousness in the Gospel according to Saint John. Here is an instance when the Evangelist matches Freud, at least Freud saying that there are times when a cigar is just a cigar. So with fish. Of course, the Fourth Gospel is a masterwork of hidden symbols and events ordered in a pattern with meaning within meaning, but John was never coy about it and certainly not morbid. There were seven men in the boat, once considered a perfect number and known to us as the number of the sacraments by which the Church spreads sanctifying grace; this can hardly have been without significance to the author who so lovingly seems to parallel the seven messianic miracles and the seven days of creation. And all this information comes in an appendix to the Gospel, not vestigially like a human appendix that can be removed without effect, but more like an ultimate thought than an afterthought. Only the Day of Judgment will put an end to speculation about these images and numbers. It is not wrong, and sometimes it is even necessary for the good of souls, to speculate about them, provided the effort is not self-serving. Any variety of equations can give the same sum; but not one of them is more than an amusing *tour de force* if you already know the sum. It is the answer, and not how they got it, that matters to John.

Doubtless, classical scholars themselves, and some great saints among them, may at first or even second reading appear to strain at a gnat in their calculations about the miraculous draft. Saint Augustine fits into the figure one hundred and fifty-three the ten commandments and seven sacraments added as a numerical series, rather like squeezing your size into a glass slipper. Or perhaps seven and ten are used as bases because they represented wholeness and perfection. Saint Thomas Aquinas is less earnest with figures: for him the number is some sort of commentary on the number of the elect. Christ's Gospel is universal, and at the time of the writing apparently it was thought, or so Saint Jerome claimed in his fanciful citation of Oppian's *Halieutica,* that there were one hundred and fifty-three species of fish in the whole world. We are not superior for knowing now that this is only a fraction of the truth; there are rectory cooks who acknowledge far fewer. By saintly precedent, we may plunder the treasury of respectable pieties and fertile auguries. One of the most compelling is the sum of all the beads in the three sets of mysteries of the Holy Rosary: one allusion overlooked by television evangelists. None of this is necessarily irrelevant or perhaps even insignificant; for God in the depths of his omniscience can layer sign upon sign without end, and, possibly in this case, he has.

Among the human certainties, though, is this: the account is not of any pagan mythic genre. Had it been part of a Babylonian myth, the fishermen would have hauled in the whale of whales, some leviathan such as men had never seen before, but not fish merely larger than usual; in a Hindu narrative, the fish would have outnumbered the stars of the heavens, but not a merely remarkable one hundred and fifty-three; or in a Zoroastrian tale, they would have been real stars and not fish at all. If the story is not made to prove a point, there is a point to the story, two points in fact, and the first point is the blatant fact that it is a fact. It simply happened. Or given the circumstances, that point is anything but simple. It is so complex as a web of circumstance and perspective that it has entangled many who have not wanted to consider its possibility; for the catch of fish points to the risen Christ calling order from the first morning light, a real man casting a shadow on land as real men cast a net on the water without any anticipation of what is about to happen. "I went to those who were not looking for me; I was found by those that sought me not" (Is 65:1).

Flinging natural prejudice aside and allowing the truth of so improbable an event, the next question concerns the meaning of the catch itself. That is the second point, for even if the quantity of fish is problematic as a symbol, and may or may not indicate some pregnant truth about how it all ties in with us today, surely there is some general message in the sheer catch. The account makes much of the size as well as the number, and the difficulty of dragging the load to the shore. This ebullience is not cheap rhetoric; John is as above such devices as is his Lord who inspires him. The ultimate meaning within any other meaning probably is indicated by the very human reaction to what happened: there is so much. A hundred fish or a thousand do not matter; counting them means that they count for something. That thing is God's generosity. It has been hinted by the jars of wine filled to overflowing at Cana, the bread left over to be collected on the Galilean hills, the measureless water measured at the well in Samaria, the earlier catch of fish that almost sank two boats long before the Resurrection. If we could count all the stars more precisely than today's awed astrophysicists, it would not impress us any more than the realization, now more certain than ever before, that they seem countless. The Creator does things on a scale whose generosity outdoes the philosophical concept of volume, so much so that it sickens selfish souls. God can give all that we desire, that we know; but that he gives more than we desire, we do not want to know. "Depart from me, for I am a sinful man, O Lord" (Lk 5:8).

Our Lord's sense of the disciple's human fright is in his appeal, "Little children", and while I would not presume to

impute whimsy to him in this instance, heaven's lofty equivalent of it is there when he calls to them about their catch,
knowing what they are thinking. And if in his oriental gravity
he had hidden his smile in the Galilean synagogues and fields, it
surely must have appeared in the faint firelight and early dawn
lashes of light, perhaps the way it may have been there when he
said in the first Easter dawn, "Do not hold me . . . " (Jn 20:17)
and in the first Easter sunset, "O foolish men, and slow of heart
to believe all that the prophets have spoken!" (Lk 24:25). So
now he calls, "Have you caught anything?", and the sound is all
solemn, in each decibel, but the solemnity is of a Solemn High
Mass sort, and solemnly droll like a father hiding behind his
back a present twice as fine as anything his children expected.

God's own Son hung in agony on the cross for salvation; he
delights now to show the fruits of redemption, gifts more
generous than we could have expected. Over the subsequent
centuries, some of the gifts peculiar to the mystics have witnessed
to this: there is, for example, the enlarged heart of Saint Philip
Neri, which an autopsy showed to have broken one of his ribs.
That was probably more than a cardiological oddity, just as the
one hundred and fifty-three fish were more than a record
mentioned in *Field and Stream.* We cannot know how these
phenomena are schemed from heaven's side, but we can say that
they are tangible ways by which our heavenly Father shows the
generosity of his love to people whose hearts and stomachs are
more persuasive than doctrines.

Pseudomysticism

A generous giver assumes a generous receiver; generosity offered
requires generosity to be received. That is true of natural
exchanges; it is the core logic of supernatural worship, which is
man's highest engagement and that for which he was made
before any other reason. The Lord who loves a cheerful giver
loves no less a cheerful receiver. He does something that would

have scandalized or at least bewildered any religion, including Judaism, before Christianity put an end to "religions" by revealing the object of all religious striving: God offers himself to his human creatures in the Holy Mass. There he is present whether or not he is acknowledged: "He came to his own home and his own people received him not" (Jn 1:10). This one phrase indicts all the atheisms of the current cultural scene, whether they are theoretical atheisms or the vastly more common practical atheisms, which are lives lived as though there were no God even by people who claim to believe in him. Christ then poignantly arraigns those unworthy communions which have become typical of much parish life: "Have I been with you so long, and yet you do not know me . . . ?" (Jn 14:9). All this goes on, yet ever is he there in the tabernacle, even in the tabernacle sequestered in some corner to make room for the thrones of clerics and the laity they have enlisted to serve them; he is really present, though his absentminded brethren walk by him neglectful of even the slightest genuflection. Really present: it is a fact controverted in direct proportion to egotistical pretensions; for the real presence of God should be no harder to believe than the real presence of ourselves, and the core modern neurosis is rooted in the fact that we are morally absent in his abiding presence.

As for the presence of God, man does not conjure him up in worship; he acknowledges God who is always there, and, by so confessing God's presence, man confesses who he is himself. That is the reason for "going to confession"; and those who say they do not have to go to confession are saying obliquely that they do not have to go to God, which is true but also fatal; and those who say that they have nothing to confess reveal that they have no God to confess to. To receive what he is, is to become what we are. And so you can say without the slightest rhetorical exaggeration that to deny God is to deny the self, and to be uncertain about him is to create a crisis of the self. All other human creations are pro-creations; we can create nothing of our own, even other human life, except for this critical denial of ourselves as his creatures. This is the diabolical contradiction of God's life-giving good and is the only way it may be said that we "create" evil, after the model of Satan, who could create nothing except his own self-contradiction.

This psychological denial of God's reality is only an enigma; it is not a mystery, for a mystery is a deep truth, while an enigma is a deep confusion. The enigma of man's denial of his own God is an artifice of the imaginative intellect, a superficial biologism that defines the self only experientially in material categories and stems from a lack of generosity in our attitude toward creation. Today it expresses itself in euphemisms, lofty sounding expressions of panic about limits of various kinds. Authorities who lack the candor to consider the possible loss of their souls speak apocalyptically about overpopulation and ecological disaster; wealth is static and the have-nots can be relieved only at the expense of the haves, and human life is a liability and not the fundamental form of wealth. Some remnant of this vocabulary seemed to set the tone even for the encyclical *Populorum Progressio* of Paul VI in 1967, though certainly not in the hapless way it informed the 1986 pastoral letter of the United States bishops, *Economic Justice for All*. The former was refined, and the latter was gracefully repudiated by John Paul II in the 1991 encyclical *Centesimus Annus*. In this teaching, the Holy Father revised some of the analysis of *Sollicitudo Rei Socialis* four years earlier and reapplied to the post-Marxist world the criteria for human dignity and authentic use of commodities which Leo XIII had considered a century before in *Rerum Novarum*.

Here was a modern example of the classical development of doctrine, with the result repudiating any critique of economic justice in the line of limits instead of opportunity. Although natural resources are not inexhaustible, they are not entirely fixed commodities; and this applies to "overpopulation", which is a zero-sum term, invalid in the light of economic realism. It is an old story; Euripides said that overpopulation had caused the Trojan War. People, and not too many of them, are the cause of war, and likewise they are the cause of peace. People are the fundamental resource for all resources, and only a static mentality considers them a burden anywhere: " . . . and although there were so many, the net was not torn" (Jn 21:11b). Even the National Research Council of the National Academy of Science, which in 1971 had warned about overpopulation in discouraging terms, changed its position and announced in 1986 that all available evidence shows no negative effect of population increases on economic growth, and, in fact: "The scarcity of exhaustible resources is at most a minor restraint on economic growth." Our Lord was not a Robin Hood when he became history's champion of the poor; he did not teach his apostles to be generous with what others have, and he went so far as to say that the lazy servant who hid in the ground what his master had given him was a moral menace (cf. Mt 25:14–28). The words should sear the consciences of our world, where much less than half of the arable land is used for agriculture.

In the many desperate economic conditions of today, where development and distribution are keys to relief, the gift of the self's ingenuity is the greatest generosity. Technology has increased per-acre agricultural yields so that, according to the World Bank, since the 1980s, world grain production has been double the annual increase in consumption. In South Korea, Hong Kong and Singapore, where there has been a steady population growth of about 1.5 percent annually, each year since 1985 has seen per-capita income doubled and the gross national product increased about 8.5 percent. Capital includes more than money or material means of production. There is not a population crisis, for people are not a liability; there is a moral crisis. Enterprise is not finite, and the risks required as stewards of God's bounty require inventiveness and use of all the virtues. Christ summoned the apostles in the boat to participate in creation by recasting their nets his way, making themselves available to his order, and nothing less than themselves. Passivity is beneath man, and any economic system that engenders passivity by some specious concept of welfare is beneath the dignity of the person as a participant in creation. "Indeed, besides the earth, man's principal resource is man himself" (*Centesimus Annus,* no. 32). All such testimony, however, will be ignored by ideologues absorbed in their pretentious little orthodoxies.

The fear of diminishing resources increases as the wealth of a people increases, and this is a perfectly understandable paradox. Juvenal was intrigued by what all the doctors of souls have known, that avarice increases with the increasing pile of gold. And as avarice is the vice of a man's declining years, so is it the vice of affluent civilizations in decline. Whatever may be the material rationale for popularized concerns about natural ecology and the distribution of wealth, without the logic of authentic Christian humanism, it creates a substitute creed of itself; and at the bottom of its quiet hysteria is a human reluctance to offer the self to the self's God. There is no telling how many scientific inventions, medical cures and symphonies might have been ours had millions of lives not been contracepted and aborted in these last few decades. In vacant spaces and empty halls, the voice of Christ, who knows what might have been, haunts the air: "Let the little children come to me, and do not hinder them; for to such belongs the kingdom of heaven" (Mt 19:14; cf. Mk 10:14; Lk 18:16). Selfishness in many ways has given us a culture of death: pseudoscientific propaganda of Malthusian ideologues notwithstanding, many industrialized countries have entered what is being called a demographic winter; in sixty-five of them, with a combined population of two and a half billion, the reproduction rate is below or barely at replacement levels. Increased population is largely due to longer life spans; the average number of births worldwide has dropped by one-third in the last thirty years. And in one cruel commentary on the selfish misuse of nature, men of marriageable age in parts of China, Afghanistan, Bangladesh, Pakistan and India are finding that there are practically no women of their age. It is one proof that people cannot break the natural law, but they can break up against it.

When this psychology of self-defined limits tries to worship, it succumbs to a spiritual cramp in the form of receptionism. This is the revealing term used in sacramental theology to describe a propensity for measuring activity by what we get without giving. The receptionist is anything but a cheerful receiver; he receives a gift as though he were the reason the giver exists. Edification replaces sacrifice. Looking back from this contemporary malaise, even the pagan religions based on sacrificial offerings, however base and bloody they usually were, probably were more insightful of the true relationship to God than are the present forms of sanitized religiosity that have replaced self-offering with self-affirmation. In self-affirmation, the criterion for authenticity is no longer the exalted object; it is a sordid preoccupation with abstract meaningfulness, by which is meant the satisfaction of a limited human expectation. Selfish people will complain that too much is required of them in worship, usually too much time, but time is the measure of life: the preaching should be briefer and not preaching at all but rhapsodies of self-congratulation, and we could easily do without all that music, especially if it is not entertaining, and the prayers should be apostrophes within the ego, and there need be no time for lingering in private thanksgiving. All this comes under the rubric that it should not take too long, which is perforce a contradictory standard for any approach to eternity; nor should it tax the intellect, even if we claim that our God is the God of Truth. The Church recently beatified a man who audaciously addressed our age: " 'The Mass is too long,' you say, and I reply: 'Because your love is too short.' "

Contemplate those fishermen in their boat on the Galilean lake and the Figure calling to them from what they thought was their homeland, and you encounter the gracious verbal ballet of God's way with his limited human creatures: in all portents, in the daily commerce of life, in the economy of the virtues, in matters touching on talent and imagination, in the sacraments and in the desire for the welfare of those we love, God gives freely, but he does not give for free. He takes the

initiative, but a response is exacted. In 1687, Pope Innocent XI
addressed what is wrong in the selfish receptionist approach as
it had blossomed into the full-fledged heresy of Quietism. It
had assumed a variety of forms, in exotic degrees somewhat
systematized by Miguel de Molinos, an Augustinian whose
confidence in the appeal of faith over human resistance was so
hymnodic that its pieties had attracted for a short while even
the man who as Pope condemned it. All sorts of movements
and cults had toyed with the same sentiment: primordial
Gnosticism, whose unreality about nature is our basic affliction,
and suspiciously modern-sounding movements like the Brethren and Sisters of the Free Spirit. Luther cobbled a whole
religion out of the distortion of faith as the solitary qualification for salvation: faith, that is, apart from moral accountability.
The Quietist engaged an entirely passive spirituality, a prayer
that was essentially a bath in good feelings, no human movement toward God and no moral resolutions in response to his
presence. Rosaries were tossed aside, the intellectual tone of the
traditional liturgy was scorned, art was suspect as too plastic for
the spiritual ethers, ritual was pedantic if it was not instinctively
emotive, doctrines of the Real Presence and Heaven and Hell
were intrusions upon the sublime passivity of the soul, and
priestly mediation especially in auricular confession was meretricious. In this self-absorption, the exactions of marriage and
celibacy equally were homeless, and sexual accountability was
a fiction of culture irrelevant to the way of love.

That was not the spirit of Galilee: "Little children!" And
John confesses a faith exacting if not yet exact, born of an
active love evident at the Last Supper and at the foot of the
cross: "It is the Lord." It is like the Mass when the priest says,
"Ecce Agnus Dei—Behold the Lamb of God", and the people
respond, "Domine non sum dignus—Lord I am not worthy. . . ."
It does not end there; adoration moves to communion when the
priest says "Corpus Christi—The Body of Christ", and each
who receives says "Amen." So it is with Peter; naked, he clothes
himself and swims to the Lord, the way the Christian approaches

his Lord by putting on the robe of baptism and the rituals of the Church in deference to the protocols of the heavenly court. Our Lord made the world, and we can fit into it properly only if we are made fit for it; creatures "put on" creation by living in the Creator's way, in deference to his order, and his commandments are his orders for being part of his order. Thus the parable of the wedding garment (Mt 22): the invitation to the banquet is generous, and we are the second-string invitees—if it is not congenial to think in those terms, there we are—and, once invited, the right form is required. Faith moves from attitude to involvement in a palpable transition. "What do you think of Christ? Whose Son is he?" was the question put to the Pharisees before the Resurrection, but after the gifting of the Holy Spirit the tone becomes more demanding and nobly incriminating: "For as many of you as were baptized into Christ have put on Christ" (Gal 3:27).

Generosity and Intelligence

We know what is meant, in that happy jargon, by a couch potato: the fellow who lounges about in a neglected state watching the ball game on the TV and boasting at the end that he won. There was something of that in the scribes and Pharisees, not in the many good ones, but transparently in those who provoked the Lord. And when our Lord watches Peter swimming toward him, he may give the impression of a sense of triumph; he has saved Peter from the degrading posture of a passive spectator to salvation. This certainly marks a change from the Transfiguration, when Peter prostrated himself, hiding himself from the glory of God. Peter then would no more have approached the glory of God's presence, the holy *kabod,* than he would have dared to approach the Inner Sanctum of the Temple, and if he had tried to do so he would have been lucky to have gotten out with nothing more than a beating from the Temple guards. But here in Galilee all is free and beckoning, and Peter takes the plunge, "putting on" a new life ordained by Christ. There are many ways Christ bids us do the same in the life of the Church, and they have come to be called precepts, though it would not be inconsistent with the experience of Peter to call them plunges, six of them: keeping Sundays and Holy Days of Obligation, keeping Days of Fast and Abstinence, going to Confession at least once a year, receiving Holy Communion at least once a year at or around Easter, contributing to the support of the Church, and observing the Church's law concerning marriage.

Peter would have been among the loudest in denouncing any suggestion of these as an artificial and optional construction. Heaven knows, and not as a figure of speech, how much harm can be done by presenting them that way through bureaucratic clericalism and mindless officiousness. The Catholic "system" is genuinely different and part of the same science of the soul that resents the unreality of passivity as much as it resents arbitrary legalism. The real system is organic, the way a human body has a system or, more accurately, is a system. Precepts, commandments, counsels, all order the soul to active life in the Church the way it is by divine design. Reluctance to enter into the system, with its obligations and exactions, not to mention its consolations and joys, may be qualified by a legitimate caution based on past disappointments with arbitrary human precepts; but reluctance to come to Christ his way ultimately issues from selfishness. The generosity of God is such that he provides six precepts for "putting on Christ" when only the single act of baptism is necessary for salvation, just as he gives ten commandments when the fundamental moral obligation is only the double commandments to love God and to love one's neighbor as one's self. Generosity recognizes in the multiplying of these obligations something more than the onerous burdens heaped on others which our Lord condemned. The great precepts and commandments come from God and are gifts, but gifts requiring affinity with the life of God to be appreciated for what they are.

The self tied up in the self will not dive into the water to reach Christ. That may be why our hesitant culture is so riddled with pathetic theories about increasing self-esteem while at the same time indulging popular psychological fantasies about transcending the self's limitations through denial of guilt and contempt for classical social conventions. The desire to "get in touch with the inner child"—by which the self delicately means itself—flagrantly coincides with abuse of children, even children still in the womb. Freedom to do what you want with your own body is the first part of the equation that denies freedom to other bodies. The delusion of such selfishness is also self-destructive. For instance, it is easy to say, "I don't want to bring a child into the world the way things are today." It is harder, but more honest, to admit that such a bromide means, "I don't want to bring a child into the world the way I am today." I cannot hope to do anything about the world until I do something about myself. Deny that, and the self can destroy the self and the world with it. The modern experience has been a textbook of this, and we are in trembling reach of an oblivion worse than modern wars and genocides, as attest falling birth rates and increasing sterility, falling moral standards and increasing crime, falling literacy and increasing ideology. Peter could have been an agent of that deconstruction had he been selfish. He could have stayed in his boat, thinking that his lake was an all-encompassing sea; and the glare on the shore would have served the office of a silent lighthouse marking the edge of the water and nothing else.

As selfishness is radical stupidity, generosity is profound intelligence. Peter was humble; that we know; and humility is generosity of mind. If we are reminded often of his humility, we are less frequently reminded that he was very intelligent. Any cursory reading of his two letters in the New Testament makes that inescapable, even for the falsely romantic who suppose that the heart exists at the expense of the brain. But counterfeit romanticism is the ground of cynicism, and our cynical society has come to the conclusion that the brain contradicts the heart and that it is brainless to have a heart. Actual brain death is more subtle to measure than heart death, but it is the definitive death biologically, and there is a parable in that. Heart transplants compel science and charity; brain transplants are the stuff of horror films. So, too, the Christian mystics habitually speak of transferring hearts with Christ, not brains; and at the Last Supper, the Apostle John did not place his head against the Sacred Brain. But this was only out of deference to the mind of Christ when it represents his divinity. As for the mind of Christ when it represents his divine will, Saint Paul says we can have it (1 Cor 2:16). Otherwise, we can be superficially intelligent, paddling about in knowledge, splashing up information, without attaining the shore. The Apostle calls this mind *adokimos,* or worthless (Rom 1:28). Even when it is at work in the think tank of some corporation or government agency, it can be as unhelpful as a brain in an autopsy pan. There are those who, as the saying goes, "have a mind of their own". Some wiser men have pointed out the pathology in that; it certainly is a mental way of ignoring the mind of Christ. Though there are limits to human intelligence, there are no limits to this kind of human stupidity.

The unaided intellect does have access to Christ, and Catholicism has defended this principle in its regard for natural theology over against the "faith alone" receptionists; but without supernatural help, it does not have access to all that Christ wants known about himself. "What do you think of Christ? Whose Son is he?" He asked it as a stimulus to the intellect, and not to defeat the audience. Bertrand Russell was at least correct in saying that, as far as he could remember, there is not one word in the Gospels in praise of intelligence. But there is much about the right use of the mind, and it is a distinction that people like Russell, who make little of the right economy of brain and heart, have never quite figured out. But Christ never explained it; he rather commanded it, as the Jews had long been commanded: "Hear, O Israel: The Lord our God, the Lord is one; and you shall love the Lord your God with all your heart, and with all your soul, and with all your mind, and with all your strength" (Mk 12:29–30).

The Lord does not give answers in his dialogue so much as he gives directions. That, after all, is what he seems most concerned about. "Cast your nets on the right side of the boat and you will find some" (Jn 21:6). He is the Truth and the Life only after he is the Way. Early on, the "system" was known as the Way before it came to be called Christianity in Antioch. What we know of the divine mind is chiefly in relation to places and events. The Way has concepts and explanations, but first it is a history, and in that history we go somewhere. In the central ceiling panel of the Sistine Chapel, the one with God the Father's finger almost touching Adam's, the cloak blowing around God is in the shape of the human brain. I do not know if this was deliberate; Michelangelo was a veteran anatomist; so, if not conscious, this may have been a subconscious recollection of some dissection from earlier Florentine days. It is too coincidental at least to be above suspicion. One thing is obvious: if the brain does stand for the divine intelligence, what most interests humans about it is that it has a plan.

For us living in time and space, this is too vital to be of passing interest. It would be of interest to know what God knows; it is far more important for our fortunes to know that his knowledge is to a purpose, and we are implicated in it. In the Sistine panel, the left arm of God gets less attention, but it explains what the right arm is doing. In the left embrace is the woman who will be the hope of the man God is creating. And as the right hand touches Adam, the left reaches toward the child Christ who will be born from eternity into infancy as the New Adam who will repair the sin of the Old. All of this is in the divine mind in the same instant, or, if you will, on the brink of the first instant. God painted this icon of Providence before Michelangelo ever lived: on the Galilean shore he engraved it with the flame of his cooking fire. As the fire and the fish were prepared before the fishermen understood what was happening, so does our Lord provide for us. He had seen Nathanael before he called him, and so he had seen Peter, and so he sees us. Then upon reaching the shore, we receive a command. Peter will take a journey to a place he does not want to go to. His only directions are to love Christ and feed his sheep. Strictly speaking, these are hardly travel tips at all. But even more strictly are they the commandments on which hang all the Law and the Prophets: "You shall love the Lord your God with all your heart, and with all your soul, and with all your strength, and with all your mind; and your neighbor as yourself" (Lk 10:27).

An Australian bishop was approached at a train station by a man who, as it turned out, wanted to challenge him about clerical celibacy. He began, "There is just one thing about the Catholic Church I don't understand. . . . " The bishop interjected: "One thing you don't understand? Just one thing? I am impressed. I am a Catholic bishop, and there are many things about the Catholic Church I don't understand." There were many things about the Church that Peter and his companions did not understand either. Which is why our Lord gently inducted them into his Mystical Body by fugitive images: the sheepfold, flock, seed, vine, house and, most telling, the Bride. When none of these images makes the mystery clearer for them, he simply fills their nets with one hundred and fifty-three fish. Fish out of the water do not age well, and they lack poetry. But there they are He could have produced one hundred and fifty-three roses, and numerous aesthetical cults would have been built around them by now. There might be even more cults if he had chosen florists instead of fishermen. There is much about it we may never understand, but what we do not know does not matter just now. What we do know is that this was planned, and the Planner called these fishermen children, and little ones at that.

All his remaining years, Peter took strength from the Voice of that first morning moment, and he urged the same confidence on the whole Church: "You will do well to pay attention to this as to a lamp shining in a dark place, until the day dawns and the morning star rises in your hearts" (2 Pet 1:19). When John, the youngest of the apostles, survived as the oldest, none of this had faded from his memory. He remembered how many fish there were, and, more than that, he remembered the Voice. He waited in his fading years for the Great Dawn, and while waiting he told his scribe to write: "Little children, it is the last hour . . . " (1 Jn 2:18).

III

THE FATHERHOOD OF GOD

Facts and Impressions

Current theological debates more often than not hardly qualify for the term, as they are emotional and subjective and political. They are not the objective exchanges expected of what properly is the "Queen of the Sciences". This is not to say that debates about theological teachings have been without strong feelings and intrigues; it would be hard to think of a tradition more volatile than that of the Church's great councils. There have been twenty-one general, or ecumenical, councils, and not one, not even their prototype at Jerusalem in the year 51, where the apostles and elders matched wits with Paul and Barnabas, was without heat. And hotter were lesser synods, like the notorious one in 897, when the cadaver of Pope Formosus was exhumed and harangued over canonical matters, he being at a forensic disadvantage because of his physical condition. When the First Vatican Council had to disperse because of the Italian political situation, it was a reminder of the older times when emperors and empresses did good and also much damage by their influences on councils and bishops. Arrangements have been modified from the early days of the Arian controversy when thousands of the local population might be massacred over the right use of a single iota. Now we fight whole wars over such lesser matters as a degree in a geographical parallel. While the outrages are deplored, the fact remains that there is a right use of a word, or even one letter of a word, when it indicates a truth of God and our eternal destiny. And if too fine a point should not be put on it, there is such a thing as a fine point; and when we admit that a theological concern can move the mind beyond matters of life and death to matters of eternal life and eternal damnation, discussion of it might even rivet our attention more than a congressional hearing on health care reform.

If you thumb innocently through a history of the Church, you could infer that certain people in ages past who used battle-axes in theological discussion must have had clumsy minds. That is not so. Nor is our generation more precise about God because it has hypodermic needles and laser beams. Look back far earlier than the councils, and you will have to admit that the Greek peripatetic philosophers who had no central air conditioning and the Confucians who had no computer chips were more cogent about the meaning of words than current deconstructionists who analyze speech the way Humpty Dumpty did. Pithiness of expression is not a modern characteristic, not in government or in the United Nations or even in all the corridors of the Church Universal. The Word was made flesh; we have become only wordy. *Gaudium et Spes,* the Second Vatican Council's Pastoral Constitution on the Church, is more than seven times the length of both dogmatic constitutions of the previous council. Although it was heralded as a harbinger of a boom so great that the Cardinal Archbishop of New York hoped his proposed designs for a new seminary would accommodate all the priestly candidates, some of its enthusiasms already have a twentieth-century quaintness; the diction certainly lacks the classical astringency of the earlier Vatican Council, which is timeless in its unconcern for being up with the times. It is quite possible that the Second Vatican Council's chief significance will not be that it was a modern council but that it was the last modern council. The Second Vatican Council's Dogmatic Constitution on the Church, *Lumen Gentium,* said important things, but it did not have its antecedent council's advantage of having been written under guns; it was more than eight times the length of the First Vatican Council's Dogmatic Constitution, *Pastor Aeternus,* which included the definition of the dogma of papal infallibility. Lord Braye wrote a tribute to the pen of Pius IX, who sanctioned that council's proceedings, and no swifter computer has yet been so honored:

> Now to this pen bow all and every pen!
> Bow Aquin, Ambrose, Austin, Origen;

While here it lies in twelve-inch case confined,
The Nations tremble at the truths it signed;
Ten thousand feathers dip and scribble still,
Incensed and ruffled by this harmless quill.

The difference between much speculation now and in classical times, or even as recently as the nineteenth century, is a difference between subtlety and pedantry. An observer may confuse the two and, sometimes out of a defensive spirit, scorn the subtle. In the golden Edwardian sunset, the affable, if slightly eccentric, Queen Alexandra used to amuse family friends at Sandringham with convincing impersonations of bright people; and the early Protestants coined the term "dunce" for Catholic theologians, who, like Duns Scotus, seemed to them to have put too fine a point indeed on theological questions. But intelligence need not be irrelevant, even if you are royal or even if you set yourself up as a reformer. We could use more of it when we presume to take up theology under modern arc lights. Just as the street crowds in Constantinople used to shout slogans with little information, you might find any audience on a television talk show doing the same. The problem now is the gargantuan ignorance of the history of the debates. Most of the theological questions considered today have some precedent; and every heresy has been addressed in one form or another already under different titles or combinations. Now, however, over 90 percent of all university students in the United States have studied no classical philosophy; they will have a hard time comparing the merits of the Chalcedonian Formula and the Humanist Manifesto. The majority of university seniors who cannot locate the century of the Civil War are unlikely to call to mind the Church's reply to Photius one thousand years before the Civil War. Unfortunately, they may have professors who tell them that there is nothing old under the sun and that every modern repetition of some mistake about God and the human condition is a unique inspiration.

One example of this at the moment is the tremendous ignorance that is brought to discussions of the revelation of God as

Father. Inevitably when grasping at straws to reject this as politically incorrect, someone will cite knowingly some simile from Scripture to argue for the opposite, saying, for instance, that Christ indicated the Motherhood of God when he spoke of himself as a hen: "O Jerusalem, Jerusalem, killing the prophets and stoning those who are sent to you! How often would I have gathered your children together as a hen gathers her brood under her wings, and you would not!" (Lk 13:34). This dazzling literalism has actually appeared in print, many times in fact, and has been received like a revelation by journalists. As a form of criticism, it is even sillier than arguing against clerical celibacy on the grounds that Christ called himself a bridegroom. It can only reveal unawareness of most of the great theological contests. The Arians relativized the sonship of Jesus to the Father (and you will find that Arius himself neglects the title Father in his *Confessions*), the Apollinarians relativized his human nature in the flesh, the Nestorians relativized his personhood in the Holy Trinity, and the Eutychians relativized his manhood. Studying their trials and errors is a grand adventure, and a humbling one, since there is hardly anyone alive who would not fall into one or more of these camps if left to solitary theologizing. That, however, is what happens to semi-thinkers who are worse than semi-Arians. Their ignorance of definitions and the history of thrashing them out leads to a mental clumsiness that would have embarrassed any slightly shaky North African bishop in the fourth century. The semi-thinker who stoops to fundamentalist abuse of Christ's appeal over Jerusalem in order to create a polemic for radical feminists actually manages to amalgamate all those wayward schools into one breathtaking heresy we might call Arianapollinestoreutychianism. Heresies should be tasted one course at a time; this one is served all at once, and any self-respecting heretic should complain.

Heretics may be humble, and they may actually exhibit many virtues, but as those virtues fall, they do so as the result of impatience, for the lack of patience is the definitive and common mark of the heretical cast of mind; if you want a quick and convenient conclusion, you will not have time to check out the history of hypotheses. As the strength of any heresy is the grain of truth that it distorts, the success of any heresy consists in combining a sympathetic cultural climate with innocence of the antecedents of the mistake. It is easier to distort the maternal aspects of God's way with his creatures, in order to create a doctrine of the femininity of God, when you are ignorant of its volatile ancient past. Cavalier attitudes toward historical precedent can turn a fact into an impression. Making fact fiction will make fiction fact. The Soviets did it through annual revisions of their official encyclopedia; our culture does it by an unwritten imprimatur for arbitrary versions of historical experience: that the Aztec Empire was a utopia spoiled by the Spanish, or that the Ptolemys were black. This can be done when history is treated as only a story, and it is a curious thing that our self-styled Age of Science has refused to respect the scientific canons of history. Once the history of God in Christ is confessed as nothing more than a "helpful story", it becomes a mythic putty that can be reshaped at will. Primitive people made idols in the shape of their bodies; neoprimitives shape their idols after their own minds. And having minds, they think not. Creeds yield to opinion surveys, and faith dissolves into sentiment. Thus the summary satire of liberal pomposity in *Absolute and Abitofhell,* after the manner of Dryden:

> When suave Politeness, temp'ring bigot Zeal,
> Corrected *I believe to One does feel.*

The world would not know about the Blessed Trinity if the human intellect had yielded to intuition pure and simple. Hinduism has an intuition of "Being, Consciousness and Joy" in the Vedanta, the supreme self-Brahman; but this is a weak impression of what heaven has to stamp on hearts and minds together as the divine trinity. At least the Hindu was grasping for truth before Christ. Confused theoreticians after Christ do something else when they replace the Father, Son and Holy Spirit with a vague trinitarianism of a Creator, Redeemer and

Sanctifier. These describe modes of being, but not being itself; and to reject the facts of being once they have been revealed in Christ is not to seek truth but to discount a truth already given. It is one thing from a distance to call Mr. Jones "somebody"; it is another thing to refer to him as somebody after he has introduced himself to you as Mr. Jones. "God has sent the Spirit of his Son into our hearts, crying 'Abba, Father!' So through God you are no longer a slave but a son, and if a son then an heir. Formerly, when you did not know God, you were in bondage to beings that by nature are no gods, but now that you have come to know God, or rather to be known by God, how can you turn back again to the weak and beggarly elemental spirits, whose slaves you want to be once more?" And then turning his face to contemporary "green" extremists who have found voices in the highest places—even the Vice President of the United States has spoken with respect for worshippers of the earth spirit—he lets forth: "You observe days, and months, and seasons, and years! I am afraid I have labored over you in vain!" (Gal 4:6–11).

Christ the carpenter carpentered the logic of his revelation in a "fearful symmetry": "He who receives whomever I send receives me; and he who receives me receives him who sent me" (Jn 13:20). To reject the Son as the modernists did at the beginning of this century, and to reject the Father as postmodernists are doing in its twilight, is to be left with a Spirit so undefined outside earthly categories that he is not called He or even Holy. But information of historical theology will remind us that the Hypsistarians and Cathari made the same mistake, and, as with them so with nature mystics now, the new "Spirit" is the Self posing as the Other. All this cultic unreality, in ancient caves or revived in modern national parks, has been the issue of the spiritualized egoism branded by theologians as Gnosticism. In its critique of life and wildlife, it has replaced the energetic classicism of Teddy Roosevelt with the animadversions of Al Gore. It can even be domesticized by cozy New England eccentrics: Mrs. Eddy, an undeniably self-empowered business-woman, denied the reality of matter in tooth and claw because it was inconvenient to the neuresthenic Self; and she just as blithely melded her spiritualism into a Mother God convenient to her Self.

Similar instincts construct a feminine Spirit of God by an arcane misuse of the Hebrew word for wind and the Greek for wisdom. As an insight, the feminine gender of these nouns is no more startling than the news that a hen is female. Saint Athanasius knew that a doctrine of a feminine Holy Spirit would make of the Third Person of the Trinity a creature, a *ktism* (*Ad Antioch,* 3, I, 616). But the Holy Spirit is not created by the Father and the Son. He proceeds from them, or is "spirated", but he is not a creature because he is God. In the eternal Son enfleshed in Christ we see the Father; in the eternal Holy Spirit we know the Father. The Holy Spirit is Christ's "promise of my Father" (Lk 24:49). When Saint Paul corrects himself and says that we do not know God, but rather God knows us, he means precisely this truth as it is revealed by him and not made up by us. It is so important that Luke makes it his climax, the last divine words he quotes from our Lord's own mouth. The Prince of Lies knows this truth and hates it, which is why he lies about it. And that Liar would have the Living Truth lie about it as he is dying: on the cross, "Father" is the first word uttered by the Lord, but in the darkest temptation to despair, which only divinity could conquer, Christ for the first time calls his Father in a cloudy way, "My God, my God."

On Metaphors

For some years the writing team of the National Conference of Catholic Bishops in the United States labored over a pastoral letter on women's concerns. It was elephantine in gestation and never came to birth, for its conception was not altogether

according to natural law. But with lucidity the writing team
did say: "Especially we must recognize the normative nature of
Christ's Revelation to us that God is our Father and hence
preserve the Trinitarian names. Such language is not merely
metaphorical. It is analogical, that is, it expresses albeit in an
imperfect and limited way the truth and life of the Trinity."
The denial of history reverses this. When truth is relative, there
is no need for analogy and all statements are metaphors. Were
that so in reality, Jesus would be, like those who twist what he
says about his Father, a cynical Master of the Sound Byte. An
age that has turned its political messages into impressions and
its politicians into creatures of image-makers, would do the
same to its God.

Images must limp when limited speech about God tries to go
it alone. East Africans call the Divine Son "the first ancestor",
and the Lakota Sioux address him as "the buffalo calf God".
These are noble terms in their grammar and far above the title
"hen" given God by matronly dilettantes. But the use of a noble
image does not mean that what is imaged is imaginary. Saint
John knew his Lord better than we do, and the intensity of his
devotion to that knowledge provoked language that would not
admit him to a sensitivity group: "Who is the liar? It is the man
who denies that Jesus is the Christ. Such a man is the antichrist
—he denies the Father and the Son. No one who denies the Son
has the Father; whoever acknowledges the Son has the Father
also. . . . I am writing these things to you about those who are
trying to lead you astray" (1 Jn 2:22–23, 26).

Misleaders have always been many, because the Fatherhood
of God is a difficult revelation, uncongenial to the native
pantheism of private intuitions. To locate divinity in the
Father and Son and Holy Spirit challenged even untutored
monotheism. If you read the sacred texts of our forerunners,
you will see at once that the Triune God was but a fragile
glimmer in the Hebrew revelation, and they were never conscious of it; the treasure given to them in shadowy language
and prophetic figures would have been incomprehensible to

them, and, in pious obedience to what they knew of God, they would have been obliged to think it blasphemous if it had been uttered clearly. As for Islam, the Trinity was why the followers of Mohammed shook scimitars at the preachers of the Gospel.

Against contemporary cliché, the Fatherhood of God is not the self-projection of Semitic patriarchalism inherited by Christianity. The Jews called God their father analogically only about a dozen times in all the Old Testament. By contrast, in the fullness of revelation the Evangelists speak of God that way at least one hundred and eighty-one times. "He who has seen me has seen the Father; how can you say, 'Show us the Father'?" (Jn 14:9). And this, too, is why the "Our Father" should not be categorized rather glibly as a classical Jewish form of prayer; surely, the structure is according to the venerable canons, but the address to Our Father would have been rare if not questionable for a traditional Jew. The Jews had a linear time frame; they were confident from experience that God was abiding with them according to a plan, and that his perfection in this scheme was so marvellous that it was unutterable; and that certainly it would have been utterly blasphemous to claim it could utter itself in human flesh. The Greeks thought in terms of a circular time frame, in which the gods had no particular destiny for them and revealed to them no laws in words by which to live; as history was then cyclical and repetitious, the highest perfection was perfect by its remove from senseless events; while the gods could be carnal as symbols, perfection had to be androgynous.

In *The Renaissance,* Walter Pater wrote not disapprovingly of the Greek gods: "There is a moral sexlessness, a kind of ineffectual wholeness of nature, yet with a higher beauty and significance of its own." He and other Victorian aesthetes would have seen something high and advanced in the present fad for gender inclusiveness in bowdlerized texts. In the Platonic system of the Greeks, it was possible to speak of trinitarian abstractions, as with the Hindus, but it was absurd to speak of trinitarian facts. Saint Augustine remarked of the Greek symbolic philosophy:

"I read there that God the Word was born not of flesh nor of blood, nor of the will of man, nor of the will of the flesh, but of God. But that the Word was made flesh and dwelt among us I read not there." Saint Paul was born in the world of the Jews and confronted the world of the Greeks and knew whereof he spoke, and when he spoke he preached:

> Where is the wise man? Where is the scribe? Where is the debater of this age? Has not God made foolish the wisdom of the world? For since, in the wisdom of God, the world did not know God through wisdom, it pleased God through the folly of what we preach to save those who believe. For the Jews demand signs and the Greeks seek wisdom, but we preach Christ crucified, a stumblingblock to the Jews and folly to the Gentiles, but to those who are called, both Jews and Greeks, Christ the power of God and the wisdom of God (1 Cor 1:20–24).

The Fatherhood of God in fact reverses self-projection. This is Ronald Knox's point:

> When we call God our Father we are not using metaphor; he is our Father in the full sense, not in some applied sense. When we call him a King, we mean that he is more of a king, not less of a king, than those earthly monarchs who share the title with him. Their sovereignty derives from his, not the other way round. So with fatherhood; it is from God, St. Paul tells us, that all paternity in heaven and in earth is named (Eph 3:15). . . . You must not wait till you can learn to understand your father before you learn to know God. It is by learning to know God that you will learn to understand your father. (*Pastoral Sermons,* I).

Twice does the Catechism say that God, who is pure spirit, "is neither man nor woman" (nos. 239, 370). God is not male, and "In no way is God in man's image" (no. 370). That which is maternal in the human order derives from him as does that which is paternal. Significantly, the Catechism does not refer God's tenderness and mercy exclusively to his maternal aspect, as have some writers. The female has no monopoly on these qualities. The image of motherhood can express God's "parental tenderness" (no. 239), but God is known as the "Father of the poor" because they are under his "loving protection" (no. 238). The Catechism also adds, with a flourish that might be helped by some further gloss, that "no one is father as God is Father." It does not say that no one is mother as God is Mother, for the divine Fatherhood has its definitive identity in the life of the Trinity. While some other religions have used the term "father" metaphorically, "Jesus revealed that God is Father in an unheard of sense: he is Father not only in being Creator; he is eternally Father by his relationship to his only Son who, reciprocally, is Son only in relation to his Father . . . " (no. 240). God is the Father who initiates the creation of male and female in his image; and the incarnate Son is specifically male (not in his divine person but in his human nature) to show us, not the Male, but the Father who made man and then brought woman from "the rib" of man as the Church is brought from the side of Christ on the cross (Gen 2:22; Jn 19:34).

When the world was a spiritual orphanage, the Blessed Trinity offered it "the Spirit of adoption, whereby we cry Abba, Father" (Rom 8:15; cf. Gal 4:5). Our nation is orphaned physically and spiritually: over half the children being born today, it is estimated, will have no father by the time they are eighteen. This has psychological consequences, especially when mothers are obliged to substitute for fathers. There are even disordered attempts to have "parents" of the same sex, as though sexuality were immaterial and sex only a circumstance; history has not known a more blatant *gnosis*. But then again, this will be lost on those who do not know the long simmering history of Gnosticism.

While "God is spirit", he can be worshipped only "in spirit and truth" (Jn 4:24). The superstition of a-historical spiritualism accounts for the barbarization of the social order. Barbarism is the worship of nature in place of God. Unitarianism refined the barbarity by professing to believe in "the Fatherhood of God, the brotherhood of man and the neighborhood of Boston", and now it seems soon to be reduced to Boston. More rural barbarians are left with Mother Nature as an analogue and no mere metaphor, and ecology for theology. Something more ominous happens when this unreality deliberately proposes itself as a replacement for Christianity. Thus, when Professor Ernst Bergmann promoted the German Faith movement by which the Nazis tried to move "beyond" Christian theology to a nature mysticism not unlike some contemporary radical feminist experiments, his creed was moist with the dew of the pagan forests: "The All-Mother gives birth to Knowing, Being, and Mind. The concept of mother-child is, therefore, the correct expression of the God-world secret. We speak of a modern nature religion when we speak of the Mind-child God, who lives in the womb of the All-Mother." When "spirit" is alienated from "truth", hysterics hug trees in half-hearted simulation of the saints prone before the one Tree on which hung the Son of the Father. The word "panic" comes from the cult of Pan, whose one revelation was revelry. And physical science can panic, too. Classical physics was nurtured in the truth of a Creator who orders his creation justly and providentially as Father. Alienated from this Father, the uncoordinated truths of science turn into hostile agents, contracepting the young and killing the old.

Something else happens, too, with a cruel subtlety. Fatherless barbarians deny the Motherhood of the teaching Church. She becomes a nominalist and bureaucratic "it". No surprise, then, when "its" priestly fathers become clerical drudges churning out problematic letters on women when they need one on men. True sons and daughters of the heavenly Father do not form committees to commiserate about the inconvenience of gender. They sing within holy Mother Church the duets of Francis of Assisi and Clare, John of the Cross and Teresa of Avila, Francis de Sales and Jane de Chantal, Bishop Carroll and Mother Seton, Pope Leo and Mother Cabrini, Pope John Paul and Mother Teresa. But when dualism creeps in, sexuality is indeed problematic, and the duet turns into a duel. Men act deaf to women as ancient Narcissus did to ancient Echo and as clumsily as modern Jean-Paul Sartre with even more modern Simone de Beauvoir. The dualist attempt at harmony is androgyny. Dualists luxuriate in the pretense that gender is irrelevant because they assume it is a mistake. It is stranger than a union of opposites; it is a confusion of opposition. The sacred dance of the eucharistic liturgy, largely lost in the static banality of the typical Mass as it is celebrated today, depicts this duetic harmony. It is a thousand pities, and a tragedy worse than a misfortune, that liturgical roles have been muddled in the name of sexual equality to the obliteration of this magnificent Christian anthropology. To justify this confusion about who will serve at the altar as though it were a matter "pastoral and not doctrinal" is to make an illicit distinction: once Christ has shown us the truth of his Father, nothing can be pastoral without being of doctrinal significance. And as we see the Father when we see Christ, no role is "merely symbolic". There are no "mere symbols" for those who have encountered the Son of the Father. Unless we want to be Gnostics again, no symbols, including liturgical roles reserved by tradition according to sexual identity, are insignificant.

The Ghostly Father

Alec Guinness's conversion to Catholicism came when he was playing the role of Father Brown. At the end of a day's filming, a small French boy thought he really was a priest and instinctively joined him along the road, taking his hand and pouring out his tales as they walked without introduction and with no thought that the priest might not understand his language. As he relates in the autobiography *Blessings in Disguise,* Guinness was moved by the confidence engendered by the universal fatherhood of the priesthood—especially as he had long thought of priests as malignant curiosities. If that filial trust is not conspicuous today, if it is sullied by scandals and prejudice, it is because manhood itself has been demeaned by a world no longer aware that it has a perfect Father. The increase in brutishness in our society parallels a decline in manly virtue. Enough realize this to have started groups that hold conferences and retreats to promote male bonding; but the model is a neurotic imitation of some Ostrogoth out in the woods making loud sounds with his body. The noble man must again arise, the manly father of the household and the manly priest at the altar, for masculinity is a sacramental of the paternity of grace. When manly grace was lacking in his own environs, the Lord Jesus stood in the midst of the awful malaise and offered his High Priestly Prayer: "Holy Father, keep them in your name, which you have given me, that they may be one even as we are one, even as you, Father, are in me, and I in you, that they also may be in us, so that the world may believe that you have sent me" (Jn 17:11, 21). The Pope has said in his letter to priests *Pastores Dabo Vobis* (no. 12): "The nature and mission of the ministerial priesthood cannot be defined except through this multiple and rich interconnection of relationships which arise from the Blessed Trinity...." When, on May 22, 1994, in his apostolic letter *Ordinatio Sacerdotalis,* the Pope explained that the reservation of the ministerial priesthood to males is unreformable doctrine, he spoke of the way God had planned it through the trinitarian relationships: "Christ chose those whom He willed (cf. Mk 3:13–14; Jn 6:70), and He did so in union with the Father, 'through the Holy Spirit' (Acts 1:2), after having spent the night in prayer (cf. Lk 6:12)."

There was a time when only bishops customarily were called Father. Cardinal Manning popularized a more general use in England a century ago. But the mediaeval practice was to call any priest a "ghostly father" when making one's confession, for fatherhood is learned by reconciliation. Contempt for the priesthood, always manifest in times of social unrest, is modernized in the clericalization of the laity, exploiting laywomen more than laymen; in attacks on celibacy and the maleness of the priesthood; but above all on the priest as Father Confessor. It is the frustration of people who have no heart for a father.

Loss of heart is loss of courage, and that is more than a matter of its Latin root. It does take courage to call God our Father because, as C. S. Lewis noticed, among other things, it means that God is not our Grandfather. A grandfather's love dotes at the expense of justice, ignoring his grandchildren's offenses and magnifying their cleverness. A father's love, by contrast, is too intimate and risked to be anything but objective and even severe. If you relegate the priest to the periphery as a "presider", you have made him your grandfather, sitting affably on a grand chair, showering smiles on his darlings who are incapable of sin. Rather than be God's grandchildren, it is better to be like that honest daughter of God in *The Horse's Mouth* who was asked why she prayed; did she not hate God? She replied that maybe she did, but he's still our Father.

Nature is interpreted maternally because she respects the initiatives of the Father. Saint Thomas Aquinas tended to equate maternal receptivity with passivity because of the biology he got from Aristotle; but the patristic witness developed in the nuptial theology of Pope John Paul II does not apply this biology to theology. Mary was not passive at the foot of the cross, and our Mother the Church is not passive in her reception of doctrine; her doctrines actively develop in her sacred tradition as does the infant in the womb. All this is part of the drama of God and his creation. Are maleness and femaleness role playing? That is the modern accusation. Yes. They are role playing. And the drama is reality, and the producer is God. If that sounds dramatic, it only helps to prove the point. To reduce gender language to androgyny means that, like the Greeks in the despond of their symbolic philosophy, we do not know the plot. And to de-sex the sacred liturgy for the sake of Orwellian political correctness is pedantry's revenge on the dignity of man and woman alike. It drags the eucharistic rites back to pagan incantations around suspicious fires whose flames are cold and shed darkness.

Ironically, the English texts of the revised Roman rite address God as Father far more frequently than the Latin texts, and in so doing they miss the deep diction of the liturgical drama. Stultifying mistranslations gratuitously use "Father" in many of the opening prayers as it should not be used, as a sentimental replacement for omnipotence and eternity. This might imply that we have a natural claim on his paternity. But we can call him Father only by adoption. The Latin texts normally do not make bold to address God as our Father until the consecration of the Sacrifice in the Canon. The English translation omits the *"Praeceptis salutaribus moniti"* before the Our Father. This neglects why Christ taught us to pray "Our Father" differently from the way he prayed "Father". He goes "to my Father and your Father", not to "our Father", for his filiation is different from ours (Jn 20:17). We are his sons and daughters by the justification of the cross. Similarly, the mistranslation of the *"Orate fratres"* misses the dialectic of the Sacrifice of the Father's Son. It is offered by the "ghostly father" at the altar and is conjoined by the active offering of the faithful people's receptivity to the fruits of redemption. This is "my sacrifice and yours". To say "our sacrifice" is a monophysitism of the Church. But there once again is a lesson from Church history not being taught.

Christ spoke most deeply of fatherhood in the Resurrection. It was then that he begins so earnestly to call his friends little children. It is days before the Ascension, and he knows what we have yet to learn: that our greatest dignity as men and women in the world is to be adopted as sons and daughters by the world's Creator, who makes his creatures his children. Saint Thomas says, "Adoption, though common to the whole Trinity, is appropriated to the Father as its author; to the Son as its exemplar; to the Holy Spirit as imprinting on us the likeness of this exemplar" (S. Th. 3, q. 23, q. 2, ad. 3) It was all of a parcel with Christ's interior dialogue with the Father, after our Lord had berated Chorazin and Bethsaida and even Capernaum for having been so obtuse: "I thank thee Father, Lord of Heaven and earth, that thou hast hidden these things from the wise and understanding and revealed them to babes; yea, Father, for such was thy gracious will" (Mt 11:25).

Nature and Grace

Self-justification never works with God the Father. It may give the impression that the self is in control, but it is self-delusion. The Father justifies us through the blood of his Son. There is a human instinct against that, as can be seen in the natural revulsion against the story of Abraham's willingness to sacrifice his son, Isaac; and once we as literary critics assume a moral superiority to God, it becomes necessary to dismiss the Son as deluded when he takes this language seriously. "The Jews tried to kill him, not only because he was breaking the Sabbath, he was calling God his own father, making himself equal with God" (Jn 5:18). At work here is a reality beyond natural perceptions, and for that reason it can even appear to contradict reality. But nothing in creation contradicts the reality of its God, and the natural order by its very order commands a respect for God who orders it. There is a natural perception which can be lovely in its reverie but only lingers as a poem, like Shelley's "Epipsychidion":

> Day and night, aloof, from the high towers
> And terraces, the Earth and Ocean seem
> To sleep in one another's arms, and dream
> Of waves, flowers, clouds, woods, rocks and all that we
> Read in their smiles, and call reality.

Obedience to the supernatural order, of which this natural order is a faint code, requires a humility that only grace can give. Much social confusion about what constitutes the moral life, or whether there is such a thing as objective morality at all, is the result of arrested development in accountability to the natural order. It does not take more than an amateur psychologist to trace this in so many cases to the absence of true fathers or neglect by inadequate fathers. Typical of the immaturity, so detrimental to the Religious Life, was a deep-seated hostility to authority and contempt for superiors. This has actually, and not coincidentally, degenerated widely into a revival of pseudo-mysticism and even diabolism. "The maturity of man begins with his acceptance of what is, or reality", as Romano Guardini wrote; and he used Goethe's Faust as a symbol of perpetual adolescents floating above facts as they complain about their fate. It should be too obvious to bear repeating. But it comes as news to a world of people who say, as Margaret Fuller said to Carlyle, "I accept the universe", without knowing the meaning of either the universe or acceptance.

Maturity requires reverence for the title of Father. Our Lord forbade us to call anyone on earth Father, as if fatherhood might be independent of God. He did not forbid the title Mother, because motherhood is endowed by nature. But fatherhood is attained by will. A female parent is a mother by the fact of conception, but a male parent is a father only by remaining with his spouse and his child after the conception. A surrogate motherhood contradicts nature; surrogate fatherhood contradicts the reason for nature. The less rational and the more animal we are, the more fatherhood will bewilder the herd and the fainter will be the great cry, "Abba, Father."

Reason might start reexamining the mystery of the pope as the Holy Father. To want a pope who is only "first among equals", a symbolic head with no gift of authority, is to ask for a Holy Grandfather. But God expects his children to be more mature than that. Moderns have been prodigal with their inheritance from God. The Prodigal Son had a parent, but only when he matured through adversity and returned to reality did he learn that his parent was a father. When Catholic sense wanes, the return to reality is the road back to the pope and bishops in communion with him as fathers. The pope cannot be understood as sovereign if he is not also understood as Father. Sovereignty is a power; fatherhood is an authority. Power is the ability to do something; authority is the right to do it. Papal authority is qualified by the divine fatherhood. And as George Mattheson wrote, "You speak of God's sovereign decrees. God has no sovereign decrees; God's decrees are all paternal. The decrees of a despot are meant to clip the subject's wings; those of the Father are meant to expand the wings. . . . Not in His honour, but in yours, does He ask the homage of your heart."

The pathos in many attempts to make the Church "more of a family" would be resolved by heeding the words of Georges Chevrot in his *Simon Peter:*

> We will not fall into the all too easy temptation of setting one Pope against another, having confidence only in those whose actions respond to our personal feeling. We are not among those who nostalgically look back to a former Pope or look forward to one in the future who will eventually dispense us from obeying the present one. . . . Therefore in speaking of the Roman Pontiff we exclude from our vocabulary any expressions derived from parliamentary assemblies or the polemics of newspapers; let it not be said that people not of our faith should be the ones who explain the prestige of the head of Christendom in the world to us.

From time to time, popes, specifically Alexander VII, Innocent XII, Benedict XIV and Leo XIII in passing, have rejected proposals for a special liturgical feast honoring the Fatherhood of God, sort of a celestial Father's Day, on the grounds that an authentic feast with a public rite should honor a mystery that occurred on a given day or a special favor. The Feast of the Holy Trinity is the exception, and there the Three Persons are honored in their unity as the source of all mysteries and favors. It is the job of popes to remind history of the historical workings of the Trinity in the Church, as it is the custom of a good father to remind his children not to neglect what they have received through their mother. Seldom is it remarked how a pope jots a "P.P." after his name in the most splendid kind of shorthand: it means Father of the Fathers, *Pater Patrum.* He is the chief teacher in the college of the apostolic fathers, the bishops. But it is not wrong, I think, to read in this a salute to all earthly fathers who, in their familial office, honor the Father in heaven by humbly reminding their children of the don'ts as well as the dos of life. Only out of limited wisdom will the child object to such information, and one gift of maturity is the ability to be thankful for being told what we did not at first want to hear. "If you who are evil know how to give good gifts to your children, how much more will your Father in heaven give good things to those who ask him!" (Mt 7:11). The Son who uttered that he knew his Father better than we do, and, out of the abundance of that knowledge, he made what might have been a question an exclamation: How much!

> Omnipotens sempiterne Deus,
> quem paterno nomine invocare praesumimus,
> perfice in cordibus nostris spiritum adoptionis filiorum,
> ut promissam hereditatem ingredi mereamur.
> (Collect for the Nineteenth Sunday of the Year)[1]

---

[1] The ICEL mistranslation of this should read: "Almighty and everlasting God, whom we presume to invoke by a fatherly name, perfect in our hearts the spirit of adoption of sons, so that we may be made worthy to enter [our] promised inheritance."

IV

ROMANISM

Samuel Dickinson Burchard is remembered for part of a speech he gave at the Fifth Avenue Hotel in New York City on October 29, 1884, in which he said: "We are Republicans and don't propose to leave our party and identify ourselves with the party whose antecedents are rum, Romanism and rebellion." Dr. Burchard, a Presbyterian minister, was a last-minute substitute for the pastor of the Fifth Avenue Baptist Church, Dr. Thomas Armitage, who had missed his train while returning from a wedding in Philadelphia. The euphonious title of their presidential candidate, James G. Blaine from the State of Maine, was the one pleasant resonance in a distinctly rancorous election. While the Democrat opponent had defended the Fenians who had been arrested for participating in General John O'Neill's raid on Canada, Blaine's own mother was a Catholic, and he ardently defended Parnell and the Irish Home Rule movement, and many Catholics who had never voted Republican were planning to vote for him in a wide sweep. Burchard's spontaneous rhetoric backfired, driving them back to the Democrats whose candidate, Grover Cleveland, won the decisive electoral votes of New York by a heart-stopping margin of 1,149.

The world then was not as small as it is now, though many of its citizens were. To those like Burchard, anything foreign was a betrayal of principles, and, with proof texts for the Apocalypse, Rome was easily the great betrayer. Rum had not come onto the scene when Saint John recorded his Revelation, but it was a problem by 1884 on the sidewalks of New York, and Rome was malarial, and it only took a flash of oratory to couple them and wrap them in sedition for pedestrian appeal.

Lord Byron had taken a happier course in *Don Juan:* "There's nothing, no doubt, so much the spirit calms / As rum and true religion." Verse like that can accomplish more in the way of honest fraternity than any number of ecumenical dialogues. As for those dialogues, some consciences in the remote future may be quickened to count the cost of their often dismal issue in these recent years. But putting the rum aside, one will have to consider at some point the long habit of the Church's sober doctors and saints, the habit of identifying true religion with Romanism.

What is Rome? Travellers' guides to her have been legion more than the Roman legions; probably more has been written about her than any city. You see, instinctively we speak of her as a woman; no one does that of London or New York. To the travel writer Francis Marion Crawford several generations ago, Rome was "a well-loved woman, whose dear face is drawn upon a man's heart by the sharp memory of a cruel parting, line for line, shadow for shadow, look for look, as she was when he saw her last. . . . " Paris is a woman, too; a blonde, in fact, says a song. But Paris is a debutante, and Rome a dowager. She knows everyone else's place, and she does not have to worry about the impression she is making; she has a long confidence born of a long life. She is in that way like Queen Victoria sitting down without looking first to see if a chair was beneath her; her younger guest, Empress Eugenie, had not been so secure, and the contrast reminded the people of London that Eugenie with all her charms was not quite what Victoria was, secure in her battlements. *"Roma non basta una vita."* A lifetime is not enough for Rome. An elderly prelate told a young priest that he would know Rome well enough after living there a year; after a lifetime he would not know her at all. But a thousand years are not enough, for Rome is a city yet not just a city. Some aesthetes love only the city, and they will dally around the Spanish Steps at leisure, satisfied with what they see. Anyone with pretensions to civilization, of course, will be stirred by fragments of what she has been to the art of living. But Saint Peter did not speak all that highly of the place. Our Lord, who knows what is in the heart of man, knew that Rome was where

Peter "would not". And that also must be some commentary on
the Romans; you cannot separate a city from the people without a neutron bomb. Peter was a Galilean, and therefore, like
Nathanael, he lacked Roman guile. Flavius Josephus described
Galileans as "courageous, good-natured, trusting, but easily
influenced and fond of novelty". They would have lost their
wallets in Rome in no time.

Over eight hundred years ago, and that is a trice removed
from two thousand years ago by Roman reckoning, Saint Bernard
wrote to Pope Eugenius III:

> What has been so notorious for ages as the wantonness and
> haughtiness of the Romans? a race unaccustomed to peace,
> accustomed to tumult; a race cruel and unmanageable up to
> this day, which knows not to submit, unless when it is unable
> to make fight.... Whom will you find for me out of the
> whole of that populous city, who received you as Pope with-
> out bribe or hope of bribe? And then especially are they
> wishing to be masters, when they have professed to be servants.
> They promise to be trustworthy, that they may have the
> opportunity of injuring those who trust them.... They are
> wise for evil, but they are ignorant for good. Odious to earth
> and heaven, they have assailed both the one and the others;
> impious towards God, reckless towards things sacred, factious
> amongst themselves, envious of their neighbours, inhuman
> towards foreigners..., they love none, and by none are
> loved. Too impatient for submission, too helpless for rule;
> ... importunate to gain an end, restless till they gain it, ungrate-
> ful when they have gained it. They have taught their tongue
> to speak big words, while their performances are scanty indeed.

The Venerable John Henry Newman repeated that in a sermon
of 1866, preaching on the political misfortunes that had beset
the Holy See at the hands of Garibaldi. Now Saint Bernard was
beyond reproach, but in the minds of his critics Newman was
not, and some of them raised their eyebrows at his commentary,
the whole of which is found in his *Sermons Preached on Various
Occasions* under the title, "The Pope and the Revolution":

The desolateness of Rome is as befitting to a kingdom which is not of this world as it is incompatible with a creation of modern political theories. It is the religious centre of millions all over the earth; who care nothing for the fickle and helpless people who happen to live there, and much for the martyred Apostles who so long have lain buried there; and its claim to have an integral place in the very idea of Catholicity is recognized not only by Catholics, but by the whole world.

A Caroline divine penned the exotic line: "It has ever been the peculiar glory of the Church of England to preserve the golden mean between the squalid sluttery of the fanatical conventicles and the meretricious gaudiness of Rome." The wonderful sentence gives every indication of being immortal, even if majestically wrongheaded. It belongs to that school of thought, now losing so many pupils, that imagines Christ having said, "Upon this rock I will found my Church, excepting the provinces of York and Canterbury." Newman was more capable of right distinctions between tastes and truths, and so like him in a more vernacular way was Ronald Knox. When asked why he never visited Rome after his conversion, Knox replied to the effect that when you have boarded a cruise ship and are feeling a little queasy, you should not go down into the engine room. You need not hesitate, however, to go down into the catacombed heart of another Rome, the metaphysical city of Peter toward which saints have cast their dying glances. And not only saints. So hapless a figure as the excommunicate Bishop Talleyrand looked to that Rome on his deathbed. The rattled conscience of this diplomat, so studied in detecting ambiguity and so careful when precision was in his interest, wanted the forgiveness of nothing less than "the Catholic, apostolic, and Roman church".

He was probably as sincere as he could be. Dying men, perhaps even especially calculating men, commonly are. The phrase was more than a legal convention. As a broken bishop but a bishop nonetheless, with indelible oils and unremovable consecrations, he meant the Church of Rome, as did the Second Vatican Council. For to say that the hierarchical Church and the Mystical Body of Christ "form one complex reality: and that this Church *subsists* in the Catholic Church" must mean that Christ *insists* on this Church of Rome. It may be regretted, it is not for me to decide, that at so crucial a time in history the Council chose so controverted a term as *subsists*. It would be quite worse if that term had been deliberately chosen because it is confusing. But the Church is satisfied that it means nothing less than what the Church has always meant. The same Council quotes Saint John Chrysostom saying that "he who dwells in Rome knows that the people of India are his members", and its *Decree on the Missionary Activity of the Church* encourages priestly graduate scholars to study in Rome to imbibe this sense (*Ad Gentes*, no. 16). When they do, they do what Saint Paul went to Jerusalem to do: *"videre Petrum"* — to confer with Kephas. Kephas, the Rock (Gal 1:18). Jerusalem was never a metropolitan see, nor was it originally the site of a patriarchate. As Eusebius of Caesarea early on described, Antioch and Rome are where Peter presided; and Alexandria claims a Petrine dignity, too, through Peter's disciple Mark. But Rome is where Peter's blood fell, sowing the seed of a tradition already vivid in the first century in Clement's first letter. He would be willful who would refute or ignore the appeal to Rome of the Church in Corinth for help in healing a schism before the end of the first century or the title Ignatius of Antioch gave the Roman Church early in the second as presiding over the Christian society.

The Roman in Roman Catholic

When Talleyrand intended the Church of Rome, he did not speak of the Roman Catholic Church. "Roman Catholic" is not of itself an ancient expression and was popularized by non-Catholic controversialists to bolster their own claims to apostolicity: if there could be a Roman Catholic Church, there could be other kinds of Catholic churches without a Roman connection. A Roman Catholic would then be merely a hyphenated Catholic. Or in some circles the term "Roman" might be used with unease as some highly strung people west of New Jersey now speak of a New Yorker. So was it used by John Philpot, an Anglican of Calvinist sympathies, who was burned at the stake by order of Mary Tudor in an early demonstration of the ministry of women. And so also did it crop up somewhat sniffingly in sixteenth-century marriage negotiations by England with Spain. Catholics began referring to themselves as Roman Catholics only when soliciting from a disadvantageous position the favors of a Protestant government, as in the 1661 "Humble Remonstrance, Acknowledgement, Protestation and Petition of the Roman Catholics of England".

Some broadminded Protestants used the term with respect. The irresistible travel diary of Anthony Trollope's energetically opinionated mother Frances has more than one tribute. Her *Domestic Manners of the Americans,* for all its criticism of American spitting habits and the like, approved of Bishop Fenwick in Kentucky, "an American, but I should never have discovered it by his pronunciation or manner". Then she observed that, because of the Roman obedience, "The Roman Catholics alone appear exempt from the fury of division and sub-division that has seized every other persuasion."

The staunchest of English Catholics in the nineteenth century, papalists like Manning and Faber, refused to speak of themselves as Roman Catholics. When the British government required the term in protocols, Manning's successor as Archbishop of Westminster, Cardinal Vaughan, objected to the Home Secretary. The feeling was so raw that, rather than conform to the government, the Catholics of England presented no public address for the Diamond Jubilee in 1897. One had been planned, but better none than one that had to have "Roman" as a restrictive qualifier. Vaughan relented in 1901 and sent a letter at the accession of Edward VII, but he was careful to explain himself to the Catholic Truth Conference at their next meeting in Newcastle: "The term Roman Catholic has two meanings; a meaning that we repudiate and a meaning that we accept." The unacceptable meaning was a Church which by being Roman is one part of the Universal Church. The acceptable was one useful for hearing today when some in our own country would speak of an American Church with the same fractiousness that formerly invoked the French Church of the Gallicans and the Austrian Church of the Febronians. Each claimed its little acre, sometimes more, allotting the pope his but not attaching to him a jurisdiction that is immediate as well as universal. If staunch papalists a hundred years ago thought the term Roman Catholic might provincialize what by its essential nature is universal, there are those today who are Catholic in culture but not in practice, who find the title Roman threatening for being too universal in its indications, or at least too foreign; it would threaten their absorption into the social mainstream, a process sociologists call "anticipatory socialization".

If "Roman Catholic" was used in a diminishing way by anti-Catholics in times past, it has become a declaration of Catholics who want to be Catholics. Cardinal Vaughan said that Roman Catholic is a right term when it "insists that the central point of Catholicity is Roman, the Roman See of St. Peter". The Roman Catholic Church is not Catholic because of Rome; it is Catholic because of Peter, who shed his blood in Rome. Where Peter is, there is the Church. *Ubi Petrus ibi ecclesia.* A council, for instance, does not have to be in Rome to be ecumenical; it does need the approbation of Peter.

Universal Rome

Besides the *Ubi Petrus* axiom, there is an official formula, one which was made a hymn in the "Nicene" Creed of the Council of Constantinople in 381: "the One, Holy, Catholic and Apostolic Church". The Church is One as she represents the divine union within which Christ prayed and the holy unity for which Christ prayed (cf. Jn 17:21). She is Holy because she is from God, and from her who is from God come her holy doctrine and holy worship and her holy ones the saints. She is Catholic by her universal mandate, which Chesterton said was too universal to be simply international. And she is Apostolic because of her organic identity with those who were sent out with the fire of the Holy Spirit on their heads and in their hearts to preach the Gospel and forgive the sins of a world so sinful that it did not even know it had sinned. All this is summed up in the often misunderstood phrase of Origen and Saint Cyprian, among many others, and defined by the Fourth Lateran Council in 1215, Pope Boniface VIII in 1302 and the Council of Florence in 1442: "Outside the Church there is no salvation." From the internationalist political model, one could take that to mean there are closed borders; but because the Church is universal in the moral way that she defies borders, this means something grander than the provincial conclusion that there cannot be salvation outside the Church; it means that there is no salvation that is apart from the Church, as the Council of Trent recognized in defining the dogma of baptism by desire outside actual membership in the Church.

This is not hair-splitting; it is, however, awareness of Latin distinctions, and these distinctions also obtain in good English, for which an increasing number of people seem to have little patience. *Extra ecclesiam* translated can mean without the Church, in a slightly archaic usage of "without" meaning "beyond", like saying Christ was crucified without the city wall. That is the fundamentalist interpretation that Pope Pius XII condemned. But it can also mean "in the absence of". Christ was crucified outside the city wall, but the wall was there. When Cardinal Wiseman in the nineteenth century wrote his controversial pastoral letter *Without the Flaminian Gate,* he was merely locating himself, not saying that he was writing it without the gate's help. There is no salvation outside the Church means there is no salvation contrary to the Church. You can be without the Church and be saved, but you cannot do without the Church and be saved. Those who understand that have a special accountability: "They could not be saved who, knowing that the Catholic Church was founded as necessary by God through Christ, would refuse either to enter it or to remain in it." Moreover: "Even though incorporated into the Church, one who does not however persevere in charity is not saved. He remains indeed in the bosom of the Church, but 'in body' not 'in heart' " (*Lumen Gentium,* no. 14). But, "Those who, through no fault of their own, do not know the Gospel of Christ or his Church, but who nevertheless seek God with a sincere heart, and, moved by grace, try in their actions to do his will as they know it through the dictates of their conscience—those too may achieve salvation" (no. 16).

The splendor of this universality is ill-served by fuzzy indifferentism: "It doesn't matter what you believe as long as you believe something." Believing that I am a poached egg will not bring me to eternal life. In a more sophisticated vein, it could melt down to universalism: "Everybody will get there eventually." The Church requires the motion of grace. "Lord, will those who are saved be few?", he is asked; and he answers neither yes nor no (Lk 13:23). He likens salvation to entering by a narrow door, and, elsewhere, he does say that those who find it are few (Mt 7:14), but his point is not, as some might have it, that you have to squeeze through it; what matters is "finding" it, that is, realizing what it is for. A door that is only for keeping people out is not a door at all but a wall. The Lord is concerned that it is closed someday forever, it will be slammed shut on those who thought they had the key and a proprietary right to it:

> Then you will begin to say, "We ate and drank in your presence, and you taught in our streets." But he will say, "I tell you, I do not know where you come from; depart from me, all you workers of iniquity! There you will weep and gnash your teeth, when you see Abraham and Isaac and Jacob and all the prophets in the kingdom of God and you yourselves thrust out. And men will come from east and west, and from north and south, and sit at table in the kingdom of God. And

behold, some are last who will be first, and some are first who
will be last" (Lk 13:26–30).

As universalism is a caricature of the Church's true universality,
so is grace underestimated by the opposite mistake of caricatur-
ing the Church's indispensability as a clubby exclusiveness.
Christ is severe in his demands, which is why the disciples
asked, "Who then can be saved?" But he is also more generous,
even to Samaritans, than the Pharisees of any age may want him
to be: "With men this is impossible, but with God all things are
possible" (Mt 19:25–26; Mk 10:26–27).

Rome is a symbol of how outrageously possible this is. Which
is why Rome can be threatening if you lack a certain spiritual
cosmopolitanism. One convert recently received a letter warning him that he was joining "the Church of the Inquisition, the
IRA, the Mafia, Al Capone, Hitler, Mussolini, Franco, Galtieri,
Papa Doc. . . . " At least the coffee hour after Mass should be
interesting. The writer did not mention that the Church has
long been likened to Noah's Ark, whose domestic arrangements would have offended most sensibilities. The Church has
many other more reputable people who might be even more
unsettling at a social gathering: from the first dead to be raised
from their tombs on Good Friday to Father Damian shuffling
on leprous feet. Our Lord did say that the birds of the air
would lodge in the branches of his kingdom; if this includes the
dove and the peacock, it does not exclude the vulture and the
cuckoo. If the Church meets with publicans and sinners, this is
after the Lord's example. There is the story of a woman strong
in the Reformation tradition who said she did not think any the
better of Jesus for his having violated the Sabbath. But the
Church is not a Reformed Christ; she commits all the acts
Christ committed and for which he was crucified. This requires
consorting with those for whom small institutions have no
room; and it requires convicting those over whom lesser tribu-
nals have no lasting authority.

As with Talleyrand, so with many who had never been

"Roman" in the first place: if they did not especially want to live as Romans, they have wanted to die as Romans. This is a negative approach, to be sure; but it is possible to reach a place backwards. Experience of ecumenical life has been long enough by now that we should be mature enough to take the following observation: Rome has an unmatched attractiveness when other attractions are fading. Few are the accounts of dying men pleading with their last breath to be received into the local Methodist Conference; unknown is the accident victim trying to stay alive long enough for one last Congregationalist sermon; it is safe to say that no terminal cynic has sought as spiritual "fire insurance" membership in Unitarian Universalism. The keys of judgment are in Rome. That is why the Devil hates and would haunt that city. There are those who say he does, but only in tribute to the aphorism that says that whenever God builds a church Satan pitches a tent across the street. He knows that if he had a heart, Rome would have broken it. So he makes do with broken heartlessness, haunting the holy because he knows better than we do where holiness dwells. The first Bishop of Rome, after all, warned us from his city: "Be sober, be watchful. Your adversary the devil prowls around like a roaring lion, seeking some one to devour. Resist him, firm in your faith, knowing that the same experience of suffering is required of your brethren throughout the world" (1 Pet 5:8–9).

An American priest has contributed an article to a national newspaper explaining why, in his view, Catholics stay in the Church. As he is the author of several scandalous novels, it was also of interest to read why he stays. He expressed affection for Catholicism's colorful stories and the naïve charm of her customs. Whether or not they are true was of little moment to him. His analysis was that of a middle-class sociologist. As for himself, he remains in the priesthood because he "likes it". That may be *New York Times* Catholicism, but it is not Roman Catholicism. Not the Roman Catholicism of Peter, who shuddered at some of Christ's stories until not even a fire could warm him. Peter did not like his priesthood. It was all satans and roaring lions and sickening crosses. Peter did not like his priesthood, but he loved it. The way he loved the Rome he could not like. It was where his Lord would have him go.

Nor has Peter's mind persuaded what once was the bulk of the Protestant world. But mainline Protestantism has practically disappeared, and it should not be unfeeling to say quietly that endowments are its embalming fluid. The evangelical sects, stronger in their commitments, nevertheless continue to fragment by their lack of apostolic order. The nobility of Eastern Orthodoxy, which, in a hoped-for reunion, has her liturgical and spiritual integrity to offer to a wider world, is obscured by the limits of its nationalisms. Against this background, in spite of turmoils and attrition and neglect of discipline, and especially in light of the role the papacy has played in the defeat of Marxism, Catholicism is becoming synonymous with Christianity in an equation not known since the early Middle Ages. There even are sceptics now glancing at coincidences on the Roman Calendar: the Pope was shot in Rome on the Feast of Our Lady of Fatima, the dissolution of the Soviet Union was voted on the Feast of the Immaculate Conception, and the communist flag over the Kremlin was lowered as the Bishop of Rome was solemnizing the Birth of Christ.

Now this creates a problem for Rome, besides the obvious one of being the target for everything that is against Christianity. The more subtle problem is: heretics today have little chance of fabricating alternative churches. Those who have abandoned their Catholic faith are inclined to remain within the structure because it is the only structure. Or, as one dissenting theologian put it, the Church has the copying machines. They do not nail their objections to the door of the church; they would rather nail their nameplates to it, and then use the office equipment.

In this they somewhat resemble the Albigensians in the twelfth century who were more of a usurpation than a schism, who wanted the castles the way some dissidents want the universities and the chanceries and the pensions. In more specific ways, the attitude resembles early modernism in targeting the Catholic

Church as the one effective vehicle for a vague new theosophy. The intellectual and cultural snobbery of the modernists at the beginning of the twentieth century had dismissed the denominations. They knew that their publicity could be secured, and their fascination to others increased, by being anti-Roman Roman Catholics. There is nothing particularly roguish about being an anti-Roman Protestant. And once Rome declares that one who was formerly her own is no longer Roman, the sensationalism evaporates and the dissenter tends to fade into the woodwork of some obscure faculty club. What at first seems in such cases to be a novel view and innovative insight turns out to have been stale all along. Anti-Roman modernism, both in its early form and in its revived presence today, has many precedents, for modernism is the antiquarianism of the self-indulgent. Upon the occasion of the suppression of the Jesuits in 1773, the Enlightenment dilettante d'Alembert enthused in a letter to the King of Prussia: "I see the priesthood married, confession done away with and fanaticism uprooted without the slightest trouble." And fanaticism as he saw it was coterminous with Romanism.

What is so of attacks on Rome from the left has also been so of attacks from the right, if we may appropriate awkward political terms only as a theological shorthand. To be more Roman than the pope is an illusion from which the utter reality of Rome has saved many reactionary romantics who see a fact when a wish glides by. The Church suffering today from arrogant modernism also knows the afflictions of some pseudo-traditionalists for whom tradition is just the parts of the past they like. This retentive impulse falls into four types that flourished in the Romantic Revival, and, because France was the intellectual and social crucible of the nineteenth century, they set their stamp there: de Maistre's identification of papal infallibility with absolute political authority, Chateaubriand's dependence on aesthetics as the critical animus of the Faith, de Bonald's opposition of tradition to reason, and Lammenais's impetuous activism, which appropriated the language of piety when convenient to his politics and dropped it when inconvenient. Mr. Dooley defined the fanatic as one who thinks God would agree with him if God had all the facts; the extremist thinks the pope is like God that way. Of course, and it is not irreverent to say so but thoroughly Roman, it is possible in some particular prudential matter to be "more Catholic than the pope"; you could say Saint Catherine of Siena was like that. But this is so in prudential decisions touching upon discipline, and not in doctrinal decisions touching upon belief. The pope may be wrong about many things that are outside the realm of faith and morals. To be unaware of that is to be like Rex in Waugh's *Brideshead Revisited.* In a catechism session, Father Mowbray asked him: "Supposing the Pope looked up and saw a cloud and said 'It's going to rain', would that be bound to happen?" "Oh, yes, Father." "But supposing it didn't?" He thought for a moment and said, "I suppose it would be sort of raining spiritually, only we were too sinful to see it." Pope John Paul II half jested with a journalist who had gushed too much: "You're too much of a papalist. If I've told you that once, I've told you twenty times." For any pope, prudence is the exercise of a private virtue; doctrine belongs to the grace of state. But if an individual takes another route and thinks that his doctrine is more Catholic than the pope's, he will not be so bold as the modernists to say that the pope is wrong; he may use the style of the old Byzantine courtiers and say that the pope has bad advisors. And so sets in that most contradictory of moral postures: a tendency to patronize the Holy Father. The condescension is like that of the baroque preacher who was giving a mission in a Roman church; he got so impassioned about the importance of baptizing infants as soon as possible that he publicly regretted the poor example Christ had set by delaying his own baptism for thirty years.

Imperial Provincialism

Because Rome is the world's uniquely universal fact, she is not leftist or rightist or even centrist. She is the universal generosity which, in a world whose little orthodoxies consist in parts of true things, is the threshold to every true thing. As Rome is too universal to be merely international, she is not in competition with nations or cultures or local churches. The Holy Father addressed this in the encyclical *Slavorum Apostolorum,* and history has known few examples of Rome's function as nurturer of culture so vivid as the struggle for the restoration of Eastern Europe. Marxism tried to fabricate an internationalism superior to Catholic universality. It is gone, and its remnants are surreal. In his waning days, Castro offered, among other devices, free symphony concerts to distract the Cubans from the international breakup. They stopped attending. To keep his eighty-two-member orchestra employed, he had them play four times a week for about fifteen mental patients in a psychiatric asylum.

Marxism never explained to the workers of the world what work is or what the world is. Rome is more real about these things and stands as a sign of the relationship between the person and culture. The reevangelization of Europe is all about an authentic Europeanism, as the reevangelization of the United States would invigorate an authentic Americanism. Pope Leo XIII condemned an unauthentic version of it in his letter to the American bishops *Testem Benevolentiae.* He criticized a cultural provincialism masking behind patriotism. What he was objecting to in part found a voice not long ago when the supercilious Priests' Council of one diocese in the "Empire State" of New York rejected use of the title "Monsignor" on the grounds that it is a foreign honor. Rome is foreign only to the barbarian. Un-Roman Americanism is threatened by the thing that is too vast to be international and too deep to be foreign. It has no language for it; it can only try to ignore it. Rome is the ghostly senator challenging from her hills any province that equates itself with the totality of human experience. Catholicism in America is too universal to be American Catholicism. But that is hard to understand when your nation is an international power. It was hard for the tribunes of ancient Rome to understand, and even harder for their provincial governors. Pilate, as the dismal records show, boasted that as governor he had power behind him and over Christ. There are many judges on the benches of our land who say the same thing, and there have been Supreme Court judges who have rattled fasces against unborn babies. All of this should have been predicted on that lamentable day when Senator John Kennedy, campaigning for the White House, assured a group of Protestant ministers in Houston that he would not allow his Romanism to compromise his Americanism. It was like saying he would not allow his lungs to compromise his breathing. But he had his pottage, and a satisfied nation walked away with his birthright.

Our nation is not famous for its fluency in languages; it has come to expect the whole world to speak its version of English. We should not be surprised when some of our compatriots refuse to speak Latin. Latin is older than English and wider than English, and that is its crime in the eyes of those who want their own empire. It indicates a provincialism that is far different from cultural integrity. Hungary used Latin in parliamentary discourse right up to 1831 as a way of being more Hungarian. Only historical ignorance, social arrogance and cultural atomism make not knowing something sound like an accomplishment. Only a theologian of such narrowness could have written in our time: "Pronouncements from Rome don't always reflect the lived experience of people in the United States." There are some experiences that should not be lived, and that is precisely why Rome makes pronouncements.

In the nineteenth century, when a naturalistic culture was challenging the political independence of the Church, the First Vatican Council issued its Dogmatic Constitution on the Catholic Faith, *Dei Filius,* whose first chapter speaks for: "The Holy Catholic Apostolic Roman Church". That Council did not intend "Roman" as a fifth mark of the Church. Nicaea was not deficient in having four. It is the fifth mark only in the pious sense that Pope Paul VI called the formative years of Jesus in Nazareth the Fifth Gospel. The adjective "Roman" is rather the link between the marks. The Church's unity is Roman and never more united than when Rome is manhandled by those who would fracture her. Her holiness is Roman and never holier than when Rome is infested by human vices that would sully her. Her catholicity is Roman and never more catholic than when Rome is shunned by pundits who would isolate her. Her apostolicity is Roman and never more apostolic than when Rome is scolded by the immature who would make her a province of their imperial egos.

Whence Cometh Tradition?

If Pius IX said that he was tradition, *"La tradizione sono io",* we can give thanks for such audacious humility. Every schismatic has said one way or another, "I am the alternative to tradition." The Bishop of Rome does not invent tradition; he locates it. During the Second Vatican Council, when an addition to *Lumen Gentium* (no. 22) was being considered, one that would say the pope is "answerable to the Lord alone", the Pope recognized that this was a fideistic and Protestant notion. Protestant, that is, because of the autonomy it gives to a personal relationship with the Lord. The Pope granted the comment of the Theological Commission: "The Roman Pontiff is also bound to revelation itself, to the fundamental structure of the Church, to the sacraments, to the definitions of earlier councils, and other obligations too numerous to mention." This was precisely the teaching of the First Vatican Council on the economy of tradition and is one in accord with all the councils.

Rome is the revelation of the revelation. Christianity is not complete if it is hidden. "A city set on a hill cannot be hid ... " (Mt 5:14). That is seven times so of Rome. Nor can Christianity be anonymous. Christ has a name, and Peter took it to Rome. And should Peter want to abandon the city, the messianic voice will thunder: *"Venio iterum crucifigi* — I am coming to be crucified again."* Each pope knows that because each pope is Peter. By the third century, Pope Saint Stephen I had a fully articulated consciousness of this. The cry went up at the First Council in Trullo thirteen hundred years ago: "Peter speaks through Rome." The pope is Peter. But the bishop of Rome is not exclusively that, though "Vicar of Peter" was an old title, used by Pope Siricius in the fourth century and by the Council of Ephesus in reference to Celestine I and by the Great Leo of himself in the fifth century. In asking a new bishop for his profession of obedience, the old Roman Pontifical speaks of the pope specifically as Peter's Vicar, and not simply as his "Successor", as does the new Pontifical. And the revised Missal prays for the Vicar of Peter in the Mass for a deceased pope. But the pope is Peter because of Christ. He is the Vicar of Christ who sent Peter to Rome. And after Peter failed in himself, Christ made him infallible in truth. Rome was founded on a wolf; Rome was refounded on a shepherd. And for all the exactions of noble obedience in the long line of Pontificals and solemn professions, it is not enough to obey the bishop of Rome. Obedience is of the pagan Latin regiment if it is not loving obedience. Saint Catherine of Siena called the Pope, even when he frustrated her, "the sweet Christ on earth".

The bishop of Rome is not Christ in the way he is Peter. In the third century, Saint Cyprian said that every priest of the Eucharist is a vicar of Christ, in the way we speak of the priest as alter-Christus; and in terms of church governance, the Second Vatican Council repeated an apostolic principle in *Lumen Gentium* (no. 27) by saying that bishops are not "vicars of the Roman Pontiff", for they exercise their power in Christ's name directly, as "the vicars and ambassadors of Christ". But it is clear that in application to the papacy, the title early on taught something very specific about the papal office. Pope Gelasius I seems to have been the first pontiff addressed as Vicar of Christ at the Roman Synod in 495, and that because he embodied the Great Commission that Christ had given first to Peter as chief of the apostles. By the twelfth century, the particular significance of the title for the pope was assumed by Eugenius III; and to object that the development of this understanding over so many centuries must discredit its apostolic authority, is to cast doubt on the very principle of the development of doctrine, a principle often invoked by the same writers who neglect it in this instance.

The bishop of Rome makes Peter present; he proclaims Christ who is never absent. The bishop of Rome is the blood of Peter and the breath of Christ. That is why Saint Catherine of Siena, like Saint Bridget of Sweden, wanted her Pope back in Rome. Not because exile would invalidate him; Avignon had some remarkably good popes in the fourteenth century, and Urban V who longed for Rome from afar was beatified. From Avignon he founded the universities of Cracow and Vienna; John XXII reformed the Curia; Clement VI sheltered Jews from attack during the Black Death; and Innocent VI condemned absenteeism, clerical luxury, and promoted mendicant orders. Exile from Rome no more prevented papal virtue than Roman residency ensured it. In the twentieth century, Pius XII was prepared to leave Rome under wartime duress, as Pius IX had been forced to do; and John Paul II is ever more widely known as Bishop of Rome, with universal and immediate jurisdiction, in travels to every other country. But Rome and not Avignon was where Christ wanted Peter, and Catherine loved Christ. Blessed Josemaría Escrivá said, "The love for the Roman Pontiff must be in us a beautiful passion, because in it we come to Christ."

This is what Vatican I meant by speaking of things Roman to a modern world. It was, as Cuthbert Butler has reminded us through the gauze of more recent revisionism, a modern council. For good or ill, it was the first council to have experience of the modern press. The electric telegraph had been invented a score of years earlier, and to this day we labor under some of the misperceptions spread by reporters at the time. The press was proud of its powers: in 1855 the *Times* of London had influenced the fall of the government over the Crimean War, quite as our press did in the Vietnam War. It thought it might do the same to the Church. Pius IX, whom E. E. Y. Hales called the first modern pope, had as attractive a personality as John Paul II and was a darling of the journalists until he refused to let them pontificate, whereupon the press attacked him as a man who had betrayed the generous social principles that were his before the revolutions of 1848. His death notice in *The New York Times* was nine lines long, on an inside page. There were statesmen who assumed that he would be the last pope. This is worth remembering when the world is inclined to assume that the enormous prestige of the modern papacy has always been so.

Vatican I did not flatter current opinion, nor did it misjudge the culture it addressed. Indeed, it was confident of the demise of liberalism as a philosophy of culture in a way arguably more prescient than some at Vatican II who overestimated the longevity of Marxism, which that Council did not even name. This possibly was part of an "Ostpolitik" that, like the treatment of Cardinal Mindszenty in the Hungarian Revolution or earlier of Archbishop Orozco y Jiménez of Guadalajara in the Mexican Revolution, cannot be included in the Church's bravest—or wisest—moments. Vatican I, like Vatican II, was followed by misunderstandings of its definitions. Even the faithful German bishops opposed a universal catechism after Vatican I, and the Hungarian archbishop, Haynald, said in words with a contemporary ring: "If a catechism is dictated to us, our sermons will next be dictated." But when Vatican I declared that the local bishops' ordinary and immediate jurisdiction "is really asserted, strengthened and protected by the supreme and universal Pastor", it repeated what Gregory the Great had said from Rome: "I do not consider it an honor that I know how to make my brothers lose their honor. My honor is the honor of the whole Church. My honor is the firm support of my brethren." No less to the East than to the West does this honor apply, as in the last century Vladimir Solovyev assured his fellow Russians, when he called Rome "that miraculous icon of the universal church".

As the Catholic Church is too universal to be merely international, so she is too ancient to be merely old. Rome is the perennial youth of civilization. Macaulay said in his famous lines that this would still be so when "some traveller from New

Zealand shall, in the midst of a vast solitude, take his stand on a broken arch of London Bridge to sketch the ruins of St. Paul's." Our Lord told Peter that when he was old he would be bound and taken where he would not. The years left Peter when he died in Rome. By the standard of the day, he was aged when Nero's rough cohorts led him across the Sublician Bridge, and tradition tells that he was too weak to finish the climb with his cross up the Janiculum along the way where a traffic tunnel now gags you with fumes. So they crucified him in his years where he collapsed. He asked to die upside down, and the Christians in the crowd wept when his head fell back. Then his face changed, flushed with blood, but changed more than that: the deep lines fled the face, and he was the young fisherman again, whose hard arms had tossed great nets. His successors keep the world young by telling his tale, one more transporting than any fantasy. The true God ordered that it be told until the end of time to all nations. Whenever clamor of one sort or another, theological or political, has tried to silence the story, one teller has kept repeating it in Rome: repeating it to Arius and Luther, repeating it to Attila and Lenin. And each time a bishop of Rome dies, however age may have worn him, the Lord of History whispers to all who call themselves Roman in a weary world: "See how young he is!"

V

A LITURGICAL PARABLE

The Hard Truth

"What I tell you three times is true." The assurance is not from the Bible. You will find it in Lewis Carroll's wise treatise of deliberate unwisdom, *The Hunting of the Snark.* The hard truth, but wonderfully hard as a diamond, is simply that what is told is not true unless it is true before it is told. Nor will a lie become true for a thousand times telling, although it will become a thousand lies. That at least, I think, is the point of Carroll's satire. He got much truth from the Bible, where in one place a truth is told three times, and it is not true because it is told three times; it is told three times because it is so greatly true that it is the publicity of the angels. The seraphim call to one another: "Holy, holy, holy is the Lord of hosts; the whole earth is full of his glory" (Is 6:3).

We seem to slip out of that golden sense of ultimate truth in two ways. The first is by losing any real awareness of the holy. The second is by denying that it has been lost. Without lapsing into criticism that would be out of place, suffice it to say that the worship of holiness is weak in our culture, and the beauty of holiness has been smudged in transmission through the revised liturgy. For without impugning its objective authenticity in any degree, its *bouleversement* of the traditional Roman rite marks the first time in history that the Church has been an agent, however unintentionally, in the deprivation of culture, from the uprooting of classical language and sensibility to wanton depreciation of the arts. Ralph Adams Cram, that singularly distinguished — if eccentric — neo-Gothicist, wrote in an essay of 1938: "Beauty is not truth, truth beauty, as has been sometimes said; but beauty is for the people an infallible test of truth, whether in art, in conduct, philosophy or religion. The ugly thing, man knows to be untrue."

107

It is immensely saddening to see so many elements of the Church, in her capacity as Mother of Western Culture, compliant in the promotion of ugliness. There may be no deterrent more formidable to countless potential converts than the low estate of the Church's liturgical life, for the liturgy is the Church's prime means of evangelism. Gone as into a primeval mist are the days not long ago when apologists regularly had to warn against being distracted by, or superficially attracted to, the beauty of the Church's rites. And the plodding and static nature of the revised rites could not have been more ill-timed for a media culture so attuned to color and form and action. Edification is no substitute for inspiration. As it is weak and feeble to say that this was not the fault of the Church's official liturgical documents but only the result of their misuse, so, of course, would it be blind to pretend that ecclesiastical arts were in excellent shape before the revisions. Cram also said of the situation generations ago that Catholic art "sometimes exceeded Protestant art in point of flatulence and ineptitude". Given his romantic Gothic bias, he was quick to trace this immobility of inspiration to the Renaissance. His is a highly disputable argument, and in making it he was only a little more temperate than Ruskin.

The diatribes of Ruskin against Counter-Reformation classicism, in the fourth chapter of the third volume of *The Stones of Venice* sound for all the world like some of our more uninformed liturgists justifying bias against the classical liturgy:

> An architecture in which intellect is idle, invention impossible, but in which all luxury is gratified and all insolence fortified; the first thing we have to do is to cast it out and shake the dust of it from our feet for ever. Whatever has any connection with the five orders, or with any one of the orders; whatever is Doric or Ionic or Corinthian or Composite, or in any way Grecised or Romanised; whatever betrays the smallest respect for Vitruvian laws or conformity with Palladian work—that we are to endure no more.

But, irony of ironies, Protestant iconoclasm turned upon the Classical and Gothic with equal vengeance, for in its heart was anger at the beauty of tradition in any form. Anything plastic in the hands of man was synthetic, and only the untouched and primitive could be endured. Cram's fair description of what happened during the Reformation in Europe and the British Isles is all the more indicting for having been written from the point of view of an architect not obliged to theological cases: "In those countries all that needed to be done was to break up the altars, shrines and tombs, to smash the stained-glass windows, whitewash the painted walls, mutilate the statues and tear down a nave here, a choir or transept there. Into the empty and desecrated shell was introduced a new type of service, barren of beauty, and the thing was done." Liturgical revision was the capstone on the barren house of worship, the croak of the canary turned into a crow. At least the English Reformation produced the sonorous language of Cranmer. Now we are left with not the remotest echo of even that.

The recent, and continuing, changes in the liturgy could not have been imagined by Cram, who, while not a Catholic, was of ritualistic Anglican sympathies. Even he would have been speechless at Catholicism's attacks on itself, assaults practically without precedent since the Iconoclastic Controversy of the eighth and ninth centuries. One small exception was the Jansenist attempt at ritual revision in the eighteenth century, which culminated in the Synod of Pistoia under Bishop Scipio de Ricci in 1786. Among its eighty-five propositions condemned by Pius VI was a familiar-sounding insistence on the elimination of side altars. As Louis Bouyer maintains in his *Liturgical Piety,* the Jansenists actually anticipated a few of the indications in Pius XII's encyclical *Mediator Dei,* such as communicating the faithful with hosts from altar breads offered and consecrated at the same Mass. But in their case, these were tainted with the arrogance of their archeologism in wanting "a rationalistic simplification of the liturgy, an exclusive use of the vernacular, and an indiscriminate rejection of all kinds of mod-

ern devotional practices (the Rosary, devotion to the Sacred
Heart, etc.)". Modern liturgical revisions aimed at a restoration
of primitive integrity, but in more than a few instances they
have promoted fantasies of what some liturgists wanted the past
to have been. They promised the Shepherd of Hermas and
produced Little Bo-Peep. And this was somewhat like the idyll
of Marie-Antoinette reenacting the life of dairymaids in her
recreation of her idea of a barn at Le Petit Trianon, the cows all
scented and her frock picturesque. Here was Rousseau's revenge
on the natural; just as the post-Vatican II period of cheap
banners and affected nonchalance and jejeune music became the
liturgists' revenge on the supernatural. The common man properly resents treatment by authorities who patronize him by
giving him what they think is common. That is his nobility,
and that is his simplicity, and that is his essential Catholicity,
which has made him at home at the Last Supper and at Solemn
High Mass, for the common man has a cosmopolitanism denied
the expert. What is common in the Church is the communion
of the saints, and that is a thing far different from the dilettante's
commonness. The Church's liturgy is properly the shared work
of kings and thralls, knaves and saints, and she is big enough for
the Sainte Chapelle of Louis IX and the hovel of the Curé
d'Ars, but her integrity has no room for the plush carpeted
"worship space" sacramentalizing the shopping mall.

   At Vatican II the Church had called for a restoration of the
noble simplicity of the Roman rite in areas where it had become
obscured; but this was what Pius V wanted, too, in 1570. Pius
XII had placed himself in that direction, as had Clement VIII in
1604 and, more incidentally, Urban VIII and Pius X. The para-
mount liturgical conservative and ritual eclectic, John XXIII,
took his course in the same line; he also had an affection for
quaint customs, though his revival of items such as the golden
straw at communion was short-lived. But as the Missal of 1962
indicated, Pius XII and his successor had been intent on revisions and not fabrications. Noble simplicity is preciseness of
intention, not bleakness of expression. It is not contradicted by
authentic ritual developments, no more than the purity of

doctrine is compromised by the development of doctrine over the centuries. But in the iconoclastic mood after the Council, free rein was given to the spirit of historicism, which was precisely the romantic misrepresentation of the past condemned by Pius XII. The Archbishop of Sens, Jean-Baptiste Languet de Gergy, had made the same point when he censured the Jansenist missal of Troyes in 1736. The problem with historicism is its ignorance of history as an organic economy. The method of constructing the Novus Ordo was like the careful research that went into reconstructing Williamsburg—academic and idealistic. And not a little dead. A liturgical enterprise like that creates a new form by archeological committees, the way Zeuxis made Venus from parts here and there. That serenely sterile creature was an amalgamation instead of a unity, a composition instead of a tradition. As a callow youth, and therefore an historicist myself, I asked a venerable college dean why he had not renovated the altar in his cathedral. He countered by asking me why the Christian Church is the only institution in the world which considers the word "primitive" good. It has taken me a good many years to recognize that this craggy Anglo-Saxon in his decanal gaiters shared Papa Pacelli's slant on historicism. Translated into the American political idiom, we might say of the liturgical decline what Henry Codman Potter said of the nation in 1889: "We have exchanged the Washingtonian dignity for the Jeffersonian simplicity, which in due time came to be only another name for the Jacksonian vulgarity."

Virtual Reality

I am afraid I am stating the obvious, for if it is not obvious as a theory it is obvious as a fact, as the terrible decline in worship attests. But to state what everyone knows can be more scandalous than to state a new idea. It is one thing to propose something that has not yet been seen; it is more contentious to call attention to what is being avoided. That is why, on the twenty-fifth anniversary of the Constitution on the Sacred Liturgy,

Sacrosanctum Concilium, which was called neither pastoral nor dogmatic, we were awash with testimonials assuring us that the liturgical revisions following the Council had been an enormous success. We were told that the new forms had withstood many tests, that they had been received with great enthusiasm by the vast majority of the faithful. The general message of self-congratulation was repeated and repeated, but in nervous tandem with official statements lamenting declines in sacramental practice and widespread liturgical abuses. It was a bit like the town crier calling, "Six o'clock and all is well. Bring out your dead." Denials of the crisis may have been repeated a thousand times three. And each of those many times, the message stared in cold defiance of facts. In *The Hunting of the Snark* it could have been true, but it finds no agent, no nuncio, no advocate of convincing voice in the world of reality. The statistics speak for themselves. Statistics may be, as the saying has it, damned lies. But they may also be damned truths. The drop in Mass attendance in the United States alone by 60 percent in the last thirty years is that sort of truth. If the changes were not responsible for the decline, they were coincident with them. And if there had been no changes, the decline would most certainly have been blamed on the unrevised liturgy. When deliberate absence from the Holy Eucharist on Sunday constitutes a mortal sin, and when this parallels a breathtaking drop in sacramental confessions, little is said about the effect of sacrilegious communions on the life of the Church. It is easier to denounce apartheid or pollution than this, if you are preaching from a suburban American pulpit. But it is not braver.

Still the stubborn denial goes on. The surrealism reminds me of the English-language programs from Albania over Radio Tirana that I used listen to with macabre fascination as a student in Rome. A staple of these broadcasts was news about military action in some village, eliminating cadres of counter-evolutionaries hidden in the hills; and each announcement would describe the joy of the local population at being freed from the threat of revisionism. And then there would sometimes be a bulletin about the accidental death of some cabinet minister who had been on the verge of betraying the revolution. As a formula, it was the same diction of all propaganda of whatever ideology, and the dissembling has been common to every bureaucratic attempt to promote an agenda. Innovations are advertised as responses to popular demand, the deficiencies of the *ancien régime* are burlesqued, and opposition is the obscurantism of "extremists" who do not understand innovative readings of the law. Thus was it in 1777 when the Jansenist archbishop of Lyons, Antoine de Montazet, arrested one of his Canons for heroically resisting renovations to the cathedral.

Overnight, up is declared down, and those who still call it up are accused of being uppity. One can only think back to the rigorous way Catholic apologists used to defend the advantages of a Latin liturgy for its precision and universality, over against the vernacularizing Protestants. Within a trice, though the world had become ever more specialized and even smaller through travel and media access, many of the same apologists shifted gears without the slightest grinding sound and defended the Mass in the vernacular as what the Church had always wanted. Their tone was that of Molière's poseur of a physician who had misstated the location of the heart and the liver: "Yes, it used to be so, but we have changed all that." It is possible that many of these commentators believed what they were saying. At least they did not bat an eye when they described what would be so if only the world were other than it is. But even in the best of cases, delusion is not inspiration. As we have noted, Cardinal Newman's harshest indictment of a man was that he was "unreal"; he would not spare the term were he alive now, though he might use a new expression and say that the current state of liturgical apologetics is an ecclesiastical form of "virtual reality".

Back to the Future

We have heard many times, without careful definition, that the human race has entered an entirely new anthropological stage. Even speeches during Vatican II spoke of it. The very thought would be more thrilling if we knew what it meant. We do know that it does not mean that we have become a species different from our ancestors. Some of the attitudes and circumstances we have been considering have had parallels in their experience. A case in point is the religious trauma of the English Reformation. It, too, claimed to its very bones that it was a thing more worthy than even a reformation: it was to be a restoration of an integrity hidden by the accretions of time and the allurements of superstition. The English reformers justified their every work in the name of a gymnastic double task: going back to the oldest times and keeping up with the latest times. It still is hard to work our way through that ideological veneer, for it has become the idiom of contemporary ecclesiastical culture.

Until recently, received opinion held that Henry VIII's Protestant children, Edward and Elizabeth, revised the liturgy out of a conscientious necessity, the former on advice because of his youth and the latter on her own initiative. We were assured that the popular response was cheers and acclamations. The Catholic Church at the time, it was understood, suffered from "religious and cultural sterility" and "arid legalism". The people were waiting for a return from Italianate religion to the true religion of the land, and when the restoration came, a hearty Tudor "huzza" went up as one from the loyal people. The account sounds somewhat of the book *1066 and All That,* which has Saint Augustine arriving on British soil and converting people painted blue to the Church of England.

In more elegant and sophisticated form, that was the verdict of the historian A. G. Dickens. Before faulting his analysis, it is only fair to examine our consciences and ask how often have we, with half his information and quality, more clumsily described the Church before Vatican II than he described his Church before the Elizabethan Settlement. Here I do not speak of the conscience in the bugaboo kind of way H. L. Mencken meant it when he called conscience "a mother-in-law whose visit never ends". Nor do I mean conscience as it is frequently invoked today as personal license for prejudice; our age has been deformed by people who have struggled with their consciences only to emerge victorious over them. As Alexander Pope said of Henry VIII's discovery of new religious principles: "The Gospel light first dawned in Boleyn's eye." A truly formed conscience is a courteous tutor to the honest mind, and, in the matter at hand, some conscientious scholars of late have been discovering a pre-Reformation Church in England far more vital than that portrayed by defenders of the liturgical deformers. In 1984, J. J. Scarisbrick published *The Reformation and the English People,* in which he provided a corrective to the politically correct defenders of the Tudor despoilers. It may be that he looked back through lenses too roseate, but he did manage to call foul to those who had distorted our picture of English Catholic life in a way similar to the misrepresentation of Spanish Catholicism in the "Black Legend". In these past several years, more balanced studies have shown the vitality of Catholic worship and catechesis, and how devastating and unpopular were many of the changes made in the name of reform and renewal. In 1992, Eamon Duffy published *The Stripping of the Altars* to this effect, and no less eloquent five years earlier was a thesis on *English Reformations* by Christopher Haigh, who rather stretches the theological imagination by calling himself an Anglican agnostic.

Much of their documentation, which forms the substance of what I would cite, consists in a representative cache of churchwardens' diaries and parish inventories. The voices of the villagers and townspeople are poignant, and their frequent distress is palpable. To study the undermining of their religion and popular worship is to revive what never dies in human nature, no matter how often we imagine ourselves plunging headfirst into whole new anthropological stages: the heroism of some who stand for principles, as more than thirty thousand Englishmen in the North did when they marched in the Pilgrimage of Grace in 1536 to protest against assaults on traditional Catholic life, conventual and lay. There, too, were the Oxford chapel riots of 1549, when scholars refused to accept the new liturgy, and the risings in the north and west. And all this was against the scarlet backdrop of the band of martyrs casting great gaunt shadows in Tyburn and the Tower, with even a bishop, if only one, among them. But as there always will be heroes, trimmers will keep coming up too, trendier-than-thou versions of Philippe Égalité surviving and exploiting the French Revolution, skilled for nothing except to accommodate error for the sake of material peace and prosperous hearths. And in self-justification, they will call the spirit of accommodation "pastoral".

> And this is the law, I will maintain,
> Unto my dying day, Sir,
> That whatsoever King shall reign,
> I will be the Vicar of Bray, Sir!

Then, undoing the virtue of the brave and outdoing the meagerness of the weak are the demagogues who terrorize the people under the guise of populism. When they engage upon a work of replacement and call it renewal, and replace a tradition with an innovation, validly or no, they tend to get testy when challenged; and testier when they are required to defend the indefensible. So they become masters of ideological seduction and political manipulation. These were the ones in the sixteenth and seventeenth centuries who looked so far back into the mists that they imagined a Church purer than a Church Catholic and said they would bring it back in response to popular cries that only their ears could hear.

When Reform Went out of Control

It should have humbled anyone to be reformed by Henry VIII. But whatever else might be said of him, Henry was conservative in his liturgical tastes, though some said his motives were mixed. In this he could sound somewhat like Napoleon, who said, to great public effect, that his first communion was the happiest day of his life and who found so much to admire in the obscure Saint Napoleon that he encouraged a national cult to him. There was an incipient madness in Henry that was not in Napoleon, and his sentimentalism was less calculating, and, for that reason, it was more dangerous; genuine sentimentalists can be the cruellest people. He might have wept when he recalled his happy pilgrimages to Binsey and Walsingham, and in his weeping he spread out his hand and smashed them. He had put rubies on the shrine of Becket and then in 1538 made himself a shrine decked in the jewels he had plundered. And Catholics went to the scaffold for keeping the devotions he had kept. But he had not planned it that way; at first his was only the cunning of the half-mad, and his reforms were meant to reflect his cautious tastes in religion. His case was against the pope, not God; and when his spirit faded, carnal disease excited his mental superstition.

In 1538, he invited the German theologians Burkardt, Boyneburg and Myconius to what we might now term a "Call to Action Conference", where they met with carefully selected English clerics, the idea being to give Henry's liturgical experiments a gloss of continental sophistication. It turned out to be not at all what he had hoped for. Haunted by many ghosts, he had wanted some pious arguments against papal pretensions; instead the Germans wanted to stop private Masses, invocation of saints and, that perennial obstacle to those who want to improve God's handiwork, clerical celibacy. Unnerved, Henry prorogued the meeting. This is not to say that the King opposed these moves by this stage in his life as violently as he would have when his motive was faith; he did realize, however, that in matters of religion it would be impolitic to move too fast, if one had to move at all. At the same time there were those, including those Germans, who let him know with courtly obsequiousness that the wisest king in Christendom might risk his reputation if he did not agree with them.

A letter from King Henry at the beginning of 1536 had cautioned bishops to show their hand only gradually. His agent and master manipulator in the work of promoting the new order, Thomas Cromwell, sent a covering letter with the King's own, repeating the advice that the people "maie be taught the truthe, and yet not charged at the beginning with over manney Novelties, the publication whereof onles the same be tempered and quallified with moche wisdom doo rather brede contention Devision and contrarietey of opinion in the unlerned multitude. . . . " Given the source, the advice was calculating in the extreme, but more calculating had been the holy wisdom of Saint Thomas More in *Utopia,* which Eamon Duffy understandably finds so fine and typical of him: "You muste not forsake the shippe in a tempeste, because you can not rule and kepe downe the wyndes. . . . But you must with a crafty wile and subtell trayne studye and endevoure youre selfe, asmuche as in you lyeth, to handel the matter wyttelye and handsomelye for the purpose, and that whyche you can not turne to good, so to order it that it be not very badde." More was martyred, though, for knowing the difference between making the best of a bad job and surrendering to it. Bluff King Hal said he was the hearty friend of the man in the street and only wanted their peace by avoiding extremes; but the man in the street knew that the most dangerous place to stand is in the middle of the road. Though Henry continued to hail the necessity of change, and to give thanks for its accomplishments, he worried privately about growing resentment in the realm. In April of 1539, his draft proclamation "for uniformity in religion" has many autograph corrections, decrying the arrogance of the people who were making theological matters their own: there were "one part of them calling the other papist, the other part calling the other heretic". In that same year, to calm the general anxiety, the King crept to the cross on Good Friday, personally served the priest at Mass and went in public procession to Westminster for a Solemn High Mass. At his death in 1547, Henry's will left over £1,200 for Masses to be said for his soul according to unreformed custom; yet the conference he had allowed nine years earlier had sowed seeds for liturgical translation that would change the meaning of the Mass he wanted offered for himself. Tunstall had summarized that conference, setting the tone for all that would follow: "The Mass is nothing but a Communion or synaxis."

From then on, that was the correct theme for those who wanted a political future. With Henry dead, the Archbishop of Canterbury, Thomas Cranmer, was free to implement the new agenda in a Prayer Book of 1549, though by calculation he would make it only a foretaste of how the unenlightened congregations were to be introduced to the new springtime of enlightened faith. According to scheme, Cranmer was careful to eliminate ritual practices only step by step, lest too many warning signals go off; he would temporarily retain some practices, such as kneeling for communion, "lest the people, not having learned Christ, should be deterred by too extensive innovations from embracing his religion". But the agenda was on track. By 1550, to ensure use of the Book of Common Prayer, all "books of old Service in the Church" were ordered to be destroyed. This was more than a modest revision. Fifty-four years later, when Pope Clement XIII revised the Missal of Pius V, his bull *Cum Sanctissimum* ordered no such destruction: while conformity was enjoined by force of law, clerics who could not afford new missals and poor publishers who could not afford to change their inventories were allowed to use their old ones. After all, the Mass is the Mass, and the Pope was not instituting a whole new order of worship. The Prayer Book revisers had embarked on a more radical project. They agreed as if by instinct that essential marks of the reduced theology of the Mass must include vernacular speech, communion under both kinds and no reference to an altar or sacrifice. In 1551, an Order in Council replaced the old altars with movable tables and ordered that a statement be read to the people explaining the innovation: "that the form of a table may more move and turn the simple from the old superstition of the Mass and to the right use of the Lord's Supper". The introduction of the table only followed other desperate attempts to diminish reverence for the Host. The 1552 Prayer Book required communion in the hand, and, while kneeling for communion was not abolished, the objections of Knox notwithstanding, a famous rubric disabused the faithful of any notion that the permission to kneel indicated adoration of the eucharistic Presence. When Queen Mary restored the Catholic worship, Roger Edgeworth recalled how the process of the reformers had degenerated: at first the priests consecrated the Sacrament facing the people with their backs to the altar, but, when that did not stop adoration, they tried hiding behind curtains altogether, eclectically reviving a venerable use but for a different purpose. "Then this way pleased not and the aulters were pulled downe and the tables set up and all the observaunce saide in Englyshe and that openly that all men mighte here and see . . . and the bread commaunded to be common brede levened with salt. . . . And then sone after were all the corporaces taken awaye to extenuate the honoure of the sacrament and laied downe on the prophane boarde clothe."

In their movements, a mix of many motives, the Tudor liturgists considered themselves to be theologians. Indeed, the term "liturgist" is rather anachronistically applied to them: it became more common with the modern liturgical movement as it enjoyed the patronage and direction of such as Pius X and the monks of Solesmes, Maria Laach and Maredsous. The Tudor liturgists were not theologians by virtue of their liturgical information; their theology, however defective it may have been, was the qualification for being liturgists. The difference marked the divide between a liturgist and a haberdasher. But in Tudor times the liturgist had so unenviable a mission that he tended to speak of his purpose as anything but what it was, the way an abortionist prefers to be known as a health care provider. And as his ranks increased, his fellows tended to be poorly informed (with the conspicuous exceptions of the later Carolines), humorless, empty of imagination, spendthrifts and last in the race that is to the swift. In the sixteenth century, two common eccentricities relieved the vacuousness of the typical liturgical reformer: idolatry of the primitive and imperiousness. Like her father, Elizabeth found these savants frustrating in politics and feline in manner. Still, they held a strange power over her. The articles of her short-lived half-brother Edward had ordered the destruction of "misused images", but under Elizabeth "all images" were to go. When she had second thoughts like her father, those who were in charge of the new worship raised a spectre of chaos if the traditionalists were tolerated. So she, who rattled a whole parliament from her throne and shouted down an armada from her white horse, pouted and cowered before the gratuitous new guidelines for environment and art in worship.

More changes were to come under this ambiguous Elizabeth. She ranks high among those in history who exempted the self from what was necessary for others. In her private chapels, Catholic liturgical appointments were kept, and the communion table stood "altar-wise". The Spanish blood in her half-sister Mary had pursued the Protestantizers like Latimer and Ridley and Cranmer himself as heretics, where she would have fomented less controversy if she had executed them for their incontestable treason. But her misplaced zeal in burning liturgists was not inferior to any modern reticence at least to stop them. One of the finest curmudgeons of the late eighteenth and early nineteenth centuries, William Cobbett, would call Cranmer "a name which deserves to be held in everlasting execration; a name which we could not pronounce without almost doubting of the justice of God, were it not for our knowledge of the fact, that the cold-blooded, most perfidious, most impious, most blasphemous caitiff expired at last, amidst those flames which he himself had been the chief cause of kindling." Once on the throne, Elizabeth was able to capitalize on the attempts of Mary to restore the old religion by fire and rack, though this policy was hers as well without the tempering prudence of a Cardinal Pole. Hindsight is an easy prophet, but it is regrettable that the executions under Mary made an easy way for later propaganda. After all, it was Elizabeth who was left to write the history of Mary, not the other way around; and Mary in all her noble reforms has gone down in the books as Bloody, while Elizabeth in all her deformations still looms behind her self-painted face as Gloriana. Elizabeth's refusal to make religion her politics led her to make politics her religion. The new Queen could be choleric about many things, but of religious zealotry for the pure sake of religion she was innocent. She persuaded herself that compromise was the definitive virtue in religion. So strongly did she hold to this that her motto might have been moderation in all things except moderation. She could kill for moderation. Her generosity was for those who presented her with the fruits of such prototypically modern cynicism: national independence, docility and wealth. The bishops were not expected to be holy or even regular in their habits; they were ordered like sheep instead of ordering like shepherds and were considered a success if their spiritual flock produced marketable wool.

The People against the Populists

In the Catholic years of Mary, statues, vestments, the great crucifixes ("high roods") and reredoses safely hidden in barns from Morebath to Long Medford had reappeared. At Mary's accession in 1553, the parish of Gratfield had all the necessary ritual equipment ready in pristine shape for the Mass; only the straw and packing had to be removed. The memory galled Elizabeth in her personal competition with Mary's memory; it goaded the liturgists in their public competition with everyone who was not a liturgist. The effronteries of the Marian restoration would not be repeated: this time Elizabeth's advisors insisted on total destruction. There would be burnings, and for moral persuasion they would be public; in the marketplaces flames consumed piles of "vestments, copes, and other ornaments, plate books, and especially of grails, couchers (large breviaries), legends, processionals, hymnals, manuals, portuesses (small breviaries for lay use) and suchlike". Officials were assigned to patrol parishes for enforcing these destructions; they could not destroy the inventiveness of the people who found new schemes for spiriting items away in hope of a better day. At Chester, one Mistress Dutton hid the Rood, two pictures and a Mass-book, and Peter Fletcher had "certin ymages whiche he kepithe secreatlye". When the tortured liturgy was enforced in 1567, nine uncooperative parishioners of Aysgarth in Yorkshire, presumably past and present churchwardens, were required to attend the new service barefoot in white sheets; then they were led out to cremate their statues, all in penance for having "conceyled and kepte hyd certane Idoles and Images undefaced and lykewise certain old pappisticall bookes in the Latyn tonge . . . to the high offence of Almighty God the breache of the most godly lawes and holseome ordinances of this realme the great daunger of our owne souls and the deceaving and snarring of the soules of the simple."

Somewhere around 1563, one of the liturgical thought police, Archdeacon Dr. Kelke, was infuriated to find that in Fillingham, copes and other liturgical items "weare taken awaie by whome wee know not"; he ordered that the Rood and other images be broken up and burned before him. In some places the people turned in liturgical books as a species of ransom, hiding others that had not been inventoried. In such matters, those in charge of the ransacking belonged to a small elite: in 1559, John Taylor was listed as one of only three in his area who were "earnest in religion". And men so earnest had much to do.

Daunted but not devastated, large numbers of the faithful continued their quiet resistance. It was reported in 1558 in Chichester that where many Rood-lofts had been removed, the wood "lieth still—ready to be set up again" along with "other popish ornaments" so that the Mass might be said "within twenty-four hours warning". Where crosses were removed from graves, their outlines were chalked surreptitiously on nearby walls as markers. Often might the laity be found attending the new services with Latin primers. John White, the Jacobean vicar of Leylan, considered "the whole body of the common people popishly addicted". He particularly objected to "Crossing and knockinges of their breste, and some times with beads closly handeled" and various practices which had to be purged from the communion service: standing for the Gospel, kneeling at the name of Jesus and receiving communion on the tongue. The Catholic churchwarden Robert Parkyn decided from experience that to use bread for the communion "such as men uses in their houses with meat" and to receive it as communion in the hand, as the Prayer Book of 1552 required, was "brought to pass only to subdue the most blessed sacrament of Christ's body and blood, under form of bred and wine".

In the village of Bishop's Storford between 1547 and 1548, vestments and images had been removed against violent objection, the walls were whitewashed, and the stone altar was replaced with a communion table. When Mary became Queen, it was not easy in such places to replace what had been demolished. The new Archbishop of Canterbury, Cardinal Pole, actually gave England a head start in some of the Tridentine reforms. Far from wanting a blockheaded reaction to past excesses, he and Bishop Bonner of London promoted the honest reforms of the Henrician and Edwardian years in preaching and lay instruction, shriven of heretical excess. They promoted the use of the printing press, beyond what the schismatics had done, to train the laity in the catechetical significance of ritual practices. That remarkable Pole, whose mother, the Countess of Salisbury, was martyred in 1541, had been created a cardinal long before becoming a priest two days before his elevation to the primacy of all England. He was said to have lost the papal election by one vote after the death of Paul III and had been one of the three legates appointed in 1542 to preside over the Council when it finally met in 1545. When the Council reconvened more than three years after the death of Queen Mary and her Cardinal, it promoted a scheme for seminaries which those two had already instituted for England. Mary and the great Cardinal died within twelve hours of each other in 1558. But that coincidence was not a seal on a great work like the death of Thomas Jefferson and John Adams on the same day; it was a melancholy signal for the undoing of what they had begun.

Pole was one of the first to implement the new instruction for reserving the Blessed Sacrament on the altar in a fixed tabernacle as we know it; mediaeval English custom had been to use a hanging pyx for reservation. A fixed tabernacle was a welcome safety measure, so it seemed, to prevent removal of the Blessed Sacrament from the sanctuary at some future date, or to eliminate reservation altogether, should Protestants regain sway. But try as they would, the Catholics of England were appalled at the damage of a few short years. When they tried to restore the sanctuaries, it was like a domestic version of the Jews come back from Babylon and comparing the rebuilt Temple to the old one: "Who is left among you that saw this house in its former glory? How do you see it now? Is it not in your sight as nothing?" (Haggai 2:3). The people of Cockersham in Lancashire celebrated the restoration of the Faith by restoring their parish church, but they complained of the carver of their new crucifix: "The rood we had before was a well-favoured man, and he promised to make us such another, but this that he hath set up now is the worst favoured thing that ever you set your eyes on, gaping and grinning in such sort that none of the children dare once look him in the face or come near him!" In Adisham in Kent, when a Protestant rector under Mary tried to keep the communion table, the papist John Austen called him a heretic and knave who had "deceived us with this fashion too long, and if he say any service here again I will lay the table on his face!"

Consequently, armed with experience, the people in many places were more caustic in their opposition to the returned Protestant liturgists under Elizabeth than they had been under Henry or Edward. The communion table was returned reluctantly to Bishop's Storford in 1559, and the chalice was dolefully replaced with a communion cup; but other ornaments were preserved until their destruction in 1570 "at the commaundement of my lord of London". The sympathetic Bishop Ferrar in

Carmarthen let the old altars be used because of "the grudge of the people", but the government's response was harsh. To prevent trouble in Essex, the sheriff was called in to supervise the removal of the old altars; and as for St. Paul's Cathedral in London, the altars were dismantled by night, so that the hapless worshippers might be met with a *fait accompli* when they arrived for prayers in the morning.

Mercenary, Worldly and Weak

In their understandable obsession with any hint of lingering Catholic piety, the Elizabethan authorities took special aim at the ornaments, vessels and hangings associated with the Eucharist. As the sanctuaries were denuded, the rectories were enriched with the altar plate. And again the prophetic voice to the governor of Judah takes on a decidedly English resonance: "This people say the time has not yet come to rebuild the house of the Lord. Is it a time for you yourselves to dwell in your paneled houses, while this house lies in ruins?" (Haggai 1:2, 4). To promote the vaunted renewal, special homilies were ordered to be read against "papistical superstitions and abuses". The innovators chose to offend sensibilities in imaginative ways: the new priest at Hacconby used the parish holy-water stoup as a trough to feed his swine, and the sanctus bell was fixed to the harness of Thomas Carter's horse. It was all done with the same snobbish spitefulness with which Voltaire's freethinking neighbors centuries later would cast their statue of him, not in any bronze, but in the bronze melted from the parish bell.

Craftsmen and their liturgical commissioners profited from the impoverishment of the sanctuaries no less than did the cooperating parish priests. At Thame, the sale of a silver cross and chalices brought £300. At the same time, parishioners were taxed for demolitions. In 1571 at St. Dunstan's in Canterbury, a stonemason charged the congregation five shillings for the favor of removing "the Idolaterous steapes of the chancell".

Sometimes the money was raised by selling the old altar stones; in St. Mary at Hill, the stone was sold for a grave. The parishioners of Ludlow were able to lay the broken altars in the nave paving so that they might be reclaimed should the nation come back to its senses. Outraged at such maneuvers, the Privy Council supplied the bishops with canned sermons explaining why communion tables were more in keeping with primitive use. Most bishops were intimidated by the arcane knowledge and political influence of the renovators and surrendered. When Bishop Day of Sussex objected, the liturgical expert Richard Cox was sent on a speaking tour of his parishes to enlighten the locals. Bishops Day, Gardiner, Bonner, Heath and Tunstall refused to cooperate and were replaced with bishops acceptable to Cromwell, Cranmer and Somerset.

Years of neglect took their toll, memories faded, children grew up in ignorance of the incense-laden ways, and Catholic opposition mellowed as officialdom equated tradition with treason. By 1590, wrote William Perkins, most of the older men and women were still papists at heart, but outwardly "it is safer to doe in religion as most doe." Even in so traditionalist a parish as Morebath, the old priest was rehabilitated by the cultural revolution and recanted his former obstinacy, publicly accepting the latest Prayer Book with formal prayers of thanksgiving. Building on the political mode of Henry, the Prayer Book had been revised in stages, so that the transition from markedly Catholic expressions to receptionism would be more palatable; with each alteration, some act of uniformity stressed that the translations contained no changes to unsettle any but the most scrupulous. At least in comparison with the even more radical Puritan worship appearing with such unexpected fervor, the Prayer Book seemed almost conservative by the late 1580s.

Though the official liturgists were small in number, their influence prevailed through official sanction and the increasing malaise of the people. Given government backing, the least informed ideologues could set themselves up as ministers of reform and local experts. Eamon Duffy summed up his voluminous study:

> The people of Tudor England were, by and large, no spartans, no saints, but by the same token they were no reformers. They knew themselves to be mercenary, worldly, weak, and they looked to religion, the old or the new, to pardon these vices, not to reform them. When the crisis of the Reformation came they mostly behaved as mercenary, worldly and weak men and women will, grumbling, obstructing, but in the end taking the line of least resistance, like Bishop Stokesley lamenting his own helplessness in the face of advancing heresy and wishing that he had had the courage to stand against it with his brother the Bishop of Rochester.

Demolishers like Philpot, Nowell, Fulke and the propagandist Foxe held to a kind of banquet-table Catholicism invoking the Catholic name without the Catholic pope or the faith of the Catholic pope. The controversialist Crowley crowed in 1588 over many ruined sanctuaries: "We Protestant Catholiques are not departed from the true Catholique religion." They were departed, however, from their altars and texts that truly spoke of holy things.

In ruined vaults old voices may still sigh for what saddened the houses of God in their day, and such sounds are a parable.

VI

NEWMAN AND LAND O'LAKES

No Variation or Vacillation

In the case of John Henry Newman, the old axiom holds: I can defend myself from my enemies, God alone can protect me from my friends. Many of the apologists for this master apologist have only wanted to make him a cipher for their own imaginings, and this had typically been the problem with modernists like the former Jesuit, the Abbé Bremond, who passed over his adamantine devotion to Catholicism as obscurantist. In the past several generations, this has set the tone in many of the Newman Centers on university campuses, where dissident voices have projected Newman as a man against the Church in a fantastic war between orthodoxy and the free intellect. Why should this surprise us when the university has been used as a repository for restless voices who could not be trusted with the guidance of souls in parishes and other places of responsibility? This is not to ignore the heroic work done by Catholic chaplains, but the long-standing mistrust of the life of the mind in clerical circles tended to view the university as a harmless place in which to place half-educated individuals, priests and religious, in charge of half-educating the young. It was like putting a match to gunpowder, and the damage done is evident in the ignorance of a whole generation that has grown up innocent of Catholic realities. Possibly by a final recognition of Newman's integrity, more than a few Newman Centers have dropped his name. Where they do still invoke him, it is commonly in support of the mistaken idea that he was against permanency of doctrine. He said that to be alive is to have changed, and to be perfect is to have changed often. But that has too often been taken to mean that all truth is changing, and not only our perception or expression of it; and that intellectual vitality is nothing more than confusion.

Newman only changed his opinion when he was not confused. And he was never confused about the changelessness of truth and its imperious command over private conscience. He was a singularly consistent man, as is seen in the slight revision of his writings that he undertook from about 1871 to 1874, when he was already in his seventies. In the first discourse of his *Idea of a University,* he properly boasts rather than confesses: "The views to which I have referred have grown into my whole system of thought, and are, as it were, part of myself. Many changes has my mind gone through: here it has known no variation or vacillation of opinion, and though this by itself is no proof of the truth of my principles, it puts a seal upon conviction and 'is a justification of earnestness and zeal'." In all phases of his intellectual and spiritual development, he was certain of this: truth is sovereign and it is objective, as both reason and will are ordered correctly only when they are subject to it. Newman's enterprise, even when he did not say so categorically, was to salvage learning from the Kantian legacy of divorce between reason and will, a contrived trauma that had hypnotized the intelligentsia of his generation and that has put the majority of educators of our own age into an epistemological coma. When authentic Catholic higher education hardly exists in the United States anymore, the experience of Newman's blighted efforts to start a Catholic university in Dublin at the mid-point of the nineteenth century may be of some help in marking what has gone wrong. His new university struggled until it merged with the Royal University of Ireland in 1882, but his lectures on the university ideal are immortal.

Whenever he wrote about the struggle of universities to keep faith with their true purpose, he tended to use remote historical examples as ciphers for his own situation. His description is even more applicable now, when the most students can hope to learn of Jesus Christ is that he was a peace-loving man with ecological sensitivities:

> Scarcely had Universities risen into popularity, when they were found to be infected with the most subtle and fatal forms

of unbelief; and the heresies of the East germinated in the West of Europe and in Catholic lecture-rooms, with a mysterious vigour upon which history throws little light. The questions agitated were as deep as any in theology; the being and essence of the Almighty were the main subjects of the disputation, and Aristotle was introduced to the ecclesiastical youth as a teacher of Pantheism.

Newman knew the cavalier attitude toward objective truth as liberalism when, as a cultural attitude, it was young and fresh; it is known by many names today even when it will not speak its true name because it has aged into disappointment and bitterness. Newman maintained what liberalism came into being by denying: the duty never to sin against the light, a claim prior to all other moral attentions. There is a silent witness to this in his austere room in the Birmingham oratory, where you can still see the Master of Arts hood from his Oxford days. The redder robes of a cardinal that he received as an old man did not replace it; they vindicated it. His lifelong commitment had been to mastering the art of knowledge. This meant knowledge as a thing sacred in itself, and valid only when it does not conjure a competition against holiness. So when brought to test, he chose to leave Oxford for a higher learning; and when he accepted the founding rectorship of the Catholic University of Ireland, it was with the understanding that he was a priest of the Oratory functioning as the head of a university, and not the head of a university functioning as a priest of the Oratory.

This is a thing to remember when now, as in the instance of Father Corcoran[1] guided by a different prejudice a few generations ago, it is suggested that Newman diminished the Catholic identity of his new university when he spoke of knowledge as an end in itself. To refute any such misuse of this "Philosophy of Severance" between learning and piety, Newman had penned an introduction to the second edition of the original Dublin

[1] T. Corcoran, S.J., *Newman's Theory of Education* (Dublin University College, 1929), lxxi.

discourses, in which he observed that he is speaking of the purpose of a university abstractly and ideally and that, as such, its object is knowledge, but that if a university is to be Catholic it will be Catholic "in all its regulations and appointments, and in its routine", and that for the sake of its Catholic integrity—although it is not required of a university simply to be a university—it should have the power to enforce "order, discipline, and religious and moral behaviour on its subjects".[2]

This is threatening language today for many reasons, and for those who have lost their grip on the meaning of Catholic education, it is even contemptible. But at the heart of the sad state of Catholic education today is the failure to note this distinction between essence (what a university has to be in order to be a university) and integrity (what a university ought to be in order to be a Catholic university). And of course this applies in general to all Catholic education at all levels and for students of all ages and attainments. The burden of his sixth discourse in the original Dublin lectures is to show that the university functions to teach the mind how to think, while its Catholic identity rests upon its purpose to manifest how right thought leads to the truth of the Faith. His listeners were reminded of the old scholastic distinction between immediate and ultimate ends. Contemporary discussions about Catholic education get hopelessly muddled when the Principle of Severance is made a Principle of Contradiction. That would seem to be the confusion in statements like one of a former president of the Catholic University of America: "We have never said that a student coming here is going to be indoctrinated. Just as a Catholic hospital is, first of all, a hospital, a Catholic university is, first of all, a university."[3]

Newman would not permit such clumsiness. Of course he disdained any attempt to make his university a place of rote

---

[2] Quoted in A. D. Culler, *The Imperial Intellect: A Study of Cardinal Newman's Educational Ideal* (New Haven: Yale University Press, 1955), 304.

[3] W. Byron, S.J., in *The Fellowship of Catholic Scholars Newsletter* 10 (June 1987): 3.

learning, but he thought that it should be a place of right learning. The misuse of propaganda does not destroy the right to propagate, nor does the preachiness of some (and today's rock balladeers outdo most preachers in their tiresomely sentimental moralizings) cancel the commission to preach, and neither then does the sad history of false indoctrination make the Catholic school any less a place of honest indoctrination. It all depends on how we respect Newman's thesis in the *Idea of a University*, which is consistent with the point he makes in the *Essay on the Development of Doctrine*. For as he made a benign distinction between a natural knowledge that is governed by the conscience and a revealed knowledge that is governed by the Church, so he holds: "The end of . . . a Catholic University or of any university is 'liberal education'; though its ultimate end may be Catholicism."[4] But this requires that we acknowledge the issue in the first place. Another Catholic university president has written: "It is of little use to approach this question of the role of an academic institution by reflecting on the 'essence' of a college or a university or a research institute."[5] Such words were not spoken to the eight Jesuits and several hundred others in the Rotunda at Dublin.

Newman first was criticized by a parochialism that could not trust an alien spirit to preserve the local cultural patrimony:

> When I have given as my true opinion, that I am afraid to make hasty converts of educated men, lest they should not have counted the cost, and should have difficulties after they have entered the Church, I do but imply . . . that the Church must be prepared for converts, as well as converts prepared for the Church.[6]

Today so great a luminary as Newman is burdensome and

---

[4] "Circular and Correspondence" (manuscript, July 21 or 22, 1852). Cf. *An Essay on the Development of Christian Doctrine,* new ed. (London: Basil Montagu Pickering, 1878), 86.

[5] W. Sullivan, S.J., in *New Catholic World,* July–August 1976, 164.

[6] Newman's Journal (January 1863), in Culler, 244.

awkward to the educator insecure in his Catholic vision, and what he says in the greatest treatise on education since perhaps Aristotle may be sacrificed for the peer approval of those sceptics in *academe* who he predicted would be the scourge of the new age. This should surprise no one who remembers that in the social annals of the modern age, the professional intellectuals have been conspicuous for their servility to trends and their lack of moral courage. Unfortunately, this has been remarkably the case in the Church, with some noble exceptions all the more brilliant for being exceptional. This must be a concern of the bishops who are the official teachers of the Church, and who are therefore especially accountable for their stewardship of the prophetic office, as the Second Vatican Council has so clearly reasserted. If there should be a bishop whose unhappy lot is to neglect the authentic teaching of the Church, his example can at least teach by default that integrity, intelligence and common sense are not universals.

Professing the Catholic Creed

Once not too long ago I stood within the space of a few days in Newman's pulpit in the University Church of St. Mary the Virgin in Oxford and in the pulpit he built for the new university in Dublin. He was the same man in both. More to the point, he had stood in both because he was the same man. His idea of a university in Dublin was only his idea of a university when he was in Oxford writ large and was a prophecy for our moment. What he said in Ireland is more than an echo of what he had said even before his conversion, in a sermon of 1841 on the definition of wisdom, and in his letters concerning the secular utilitarianism of Peel's Tamworth Reading Room address.

The Catholic Creed is one whole, and Philosophy again is one whole; each may be compared to an individual to which nothing can be added, from which nothing can be taken away. They may be professed, but there is no middle ground between professing and not professing. A University, so called, which refuses to profess the Catholic Creed, is, from the nature of the case, hostile both to the Church and to Philosophy.[7]

A theory had not been refined by fire; a theory had been tested by fire. In our own day it has nearly been destroyed by fire. And this is because we have not been lacking modern Catholic teachers oblivious to the kind of confidence Newman had in the superiority of the liberal arts to specious liberalism, or what he associated with Bentham's artless concept of personal liberty as the guarantor of the greatest happiness for the greatest number. It has been a clerical fault, and a few signs of hope today seem to be principally in lay initiatives. Newman would have expected as much, and he urged as much. When he refused to involve himself in a controversy surrounding Gladstone's Irish University Bill of 1873, he remembered how one of his chief problems with the Irish University twenty years earlier had been clerical abuse of the lay intellect: "The laity have been disgusted and become infidel, and only two parties exist, both ultras in opposite directions."[8]

One might describe the same today, though the clericalization of the laity that Newman abhorred has also come to mean a laicization of the clergy. But the problem of infidelity remains. And of it the most important lesson is its definition. For Newman was not content to think that fidelity could consist in less than obedience to the See of Peter. In 1851 he was one of three

[7] *My Campaign in Ireland,* part 1. *Catholic University Reports and Other Papers* (Aberdeen: A. King, 1896), 270. Cf. *Fifteen Sermons Preached before the University of Oxford, 1826–1843* (London: Longman, Green and Co., 1871), sermon 14. See also letters on the Tamworth Reading Room address, reprinted in *Discussions and Arguments on Various Subjects* (London: Longman, Green and Co., 1885).

[8] Newman to Mr. Fottrell (December 10, 1873), in W. Ward, *The Life of John Henry Cardinal Newman* (London: Longman, Green and Co., 1912), 2:397.

members of a commission that prepared a report on the organization of the proposed Catholic University of Ireland: all officers and professors of the University must make "a Profession of the Catholic Faith according to the form of Pope Pius IV". Moreover, they were required "not only not to teach anything contrary to Religion, but to take advantage of the occasion the subjects they treat of may offer, to point out that Religion is the basis of Science, and to inculcate the love of Religion and its duties."[9] To be learned in a Catholic way means to understand that such obedience is not an abandonment of the life of the mind but is its freest expression. In the jargon of modern Catholic education, academic freedom has come to mean academic independence from this higher economy. The pursuit of wisdom, which is the maturity of a life intent on truth, has been replaced by the pursuit of sophistry; and sophistry marks the immaturity of a life intent on utility: not "Is it good?", but "What is it good for?" He continues in words only more unsettling for having been written over a century ago:

> You will be doing the greatest possible benefit to the Catholic cause all over the world, if you succeed in making the University a middle station at which laity and clergy can meet, so as to learn to understand and yield to each other, and from which, as from a common ground, they may act in union upon an age which is running headlong into infidelity, and however evil in themselves may be the men and the measures which of late years have had so great a success against the Holy See, they will in the Providence of God be made the instruments of good, if they teach us that the "obsequium" which the laity owe religion is "rationabile".[10]

So his motive for the presence of laymen as university officers is a far cry from the college president who said recently: "In the 1960s and early 1970s most Catholic colleges severed even tenuous ties to the Church.... We became independent

---

[9] *My Campaign in Ireland*, 80.
[10] Newman to Mr. Fottrell (December 10, 1873), in Ward, 2:398.

and named lay trustees because of accreditation, the increased sophistication of higher education as a major enterprise and because of the demands of growth."[11]Newman spoke of another economy to which such gaucherie is oblivious: "I want the educated layman to be religious and the devout ecclesiastic to be intellectual."[12] He feared, and his fear was not paranoia but prophecy, that the clericalization of the laity would only make them unfit for being Catholic in a world that has more laymen than clergymen. He saw that the ground of modern discontent is not a *trahison des laïcs;* it is a *trahison des clercs.* The more people are clericalized, the more people are likely to be involved in the treason. He spoke when clericalism was constituted by a defensive reaction against the spirit of indifferentism; today it is almost synonymous with its embrace. But both represent a lack of confidence in the ability of true philosophy to civilize man.

By "philosophy" Newman has settled upon a difficult translation of the Greek *arete:* "wisdom" is not adequate, as it "has a direct relation to conduct and human life", nor do words like "knowledge" and "science" and "judgment" convey the sense of something more than intellectual facility. For all its ambiguity, "philosophy" is chosen in the sixth discourse as the cipher for an "ordering power", a reason exercised upon knowledge. It is the enlargement, or illumination, of the mind that cracks the egghead, dismantles the ivory tower, exposes the uselessness of utilitarianism and enables wisdom "to meet the great infidel &c. questions of the day".[13] The clerical modernist, no more than the clerical reactionary, can permit this philosophy and

[11] Sister Bridgid Driscoll, quoted in *Education: Suburban People's Spring Supplement,* January 11, 1987.

[12] Ward, 2:395.

[13] Newman's Journal (January 1863), in Culler, 244. Cf. *The Idea of a University Defined and Illustrated* (London: Longman, Green and Co., 1929), 133ff. The fourteenth of the *Fifteen Sermons Preached before the University of Oxford,* 1836–1843 simply equates wisdom with philosophy. By enlarging upon the distinction in the sixth discourse, Newman intends no contradiction; he would consider philosophy more in terms of the intellect than of behavior.

hope to perdure, for it is a habit of the mind that sees through ideology. Philosophy is the endowment conferred when mere instruction yields to education. And an institution does not educate that does not cultivate it.

Newman's account of the mentality that cannot comprehend the realities of culture applies to the modernist who today rebels against attempts by the Holy See to reform the nominally Catholic universities precisely as in his time it described the pedantry of reaction and liberalism alike. Modernism, after all, is pedantic, as it myopically perceives tradition and development. Newman understood its antecedents as refuges from reality. Modernism can continue to exist only as an anachronistic nostalgia for Victorian optimism. As a result, academic freedom means for the modernist a guarantee of domain for ideology over philosophy, or what has come to be called political correctness. In his *Letter to the Duke of Norfolk,* Newman will describe the late-twentieth-century academic scene with unnerving preciseness: "All through my day, there has been a resolute warfare, I had almost said conspiracy, against the rights of conscience, as I have described it. (Learning) and science have been embodied in great institutions in order to put it down. Noble buildings have been reared as fortresses against that spiritual, invisible influence which is too subtle for science. . . . Chairs in Universities have been made the seats of an antagonist tradition." The basic right of conscience is the right to be right and not a mere sentiment; conscience is a "stern monitor" and not a *carte blanche.* The Church protects conscience as does no lesser institution, including the university, because she knows what properly forms the conscience. When some voice from the academic grove says "I feel", shades of all the Church's doctors answer "We think." The authentically formed conscience is the ground of intellectual freedom; "pick-and-choose" Catholicism justifies itself by invoking an illusory freedom. Attacks on conscience in the name of conscience, in Catholic universities themselves, posture in academic dress to cloak an anti-intellectualism far more otiose than that which Newman would expose among the English Catholics of his day:

> From their very blindness [they] cannot see that they are blind. To aim then at improving the condition, the status, of the Catholic body, by a careful survey of their argumentative basis, of their position relatively to the philosophy and the character of the day, by giving them juster views by enlarging and refining their minds, in one word, by education, is (in their view) more than a superficiality or a hobby—it is an insult. It implies that they are deficient in material points.[14]

The Irish Circumstance

At the Roman Synod on the Laity in 1987, the Father General of the Society of Jesus, Father Kolvenbach, remarked "a certain discouragement, almost a sense of desperation, regarding the possibility of assuring educational institutions of a clear Catholic identity". Two years later he defined that identity with a Newmanian sympathy as he spoke at Georgetown University:

> In a Jesuit college or university the knowledge of the whole of reality remains incomplete and to that extent untrue, without the knowledge of the humanizing incarnation of God in Christ and the divinizing of men and women by the gift of the Spirit. Transfiguration of [sic] Christ by the power of the Spirit is part of human reality itself. This transfiguration, which continues among us, saves us even as it calls us to integrate all learning and all science. It is this transfiguration which makes the work of a Jesuit university a project and an adventure that is both human and divine, one which proclaims that in spite of the prodigious diversity of technologies and the centrifugal forces at work in many areas of learning,

---

[14] Newman's Journal (January 1863), in Culler, 244.

the idea of a university, which is the integral realization of the human person, is revealed to us as possible.[15]

Newman boasted that the Church had an influence in his day over her institutions that she had not in the twelfth and thirteenth centuries; and this clear refinement of Catholic identity made it easier to fight unbelief. But we cannot say now what Newman was glad to say then: "Secular advantages no longer present an inducement to hypocrisy and [the university's] members in consequence have the consolation of being able to be sure of each other."[16]

If the Irish bishops were not desperate about Catholic identity in 1850, when Newman was about to be approached about the rectorship of the university to be established in Dublin, they were divided on the question of how to secure it. The Archbishop of Dublin, Dr. Murray, had wanted some form of cooperation with the Queen's Colleges of Sir Robert Peel's scheme. The colleges were the attempt of a worthy man in a politically volatile situation to build upon the provisions of the Catholic Relief Act of 1793; he hoped to give Catholics wider access to degrees through the model of nonsectarian systems in France and Germany. They were what we should call secular schools and were quite in keeping with Peel's pragmatism, though they did not sit well with his aversion to any state control of education. They were the opposite of Newman's idea of a university. Peel had honestly attempted a solution and could cite the precedent of the National Education Act of 1831, which dealt with primary education. But this act for "mixed education" had already failed in practice; and neither the manifest good will of Lord Clarendon, viceroy for Ireland, nor the arbitrations of the Catholic bishops of Ireland could allay doubts. The nationalist Young Irelanders favored the plan, though this

[15] The Very Rev. Peter-Hans Kolvenbach, in "Seventh Ordinary General Assembly", *L'Osservatore Romano,* English ed., November 9, 1987; and *First Things,* March 1990.

[16] Newman to J. R. Mozley (October 24, 1881), in Ward, 2:518.

did anything but inspire the confidence of those Irish hierarchs who regarded them as morally questionable "Mazzinian" enemies of the Faith. O'Connell characteristically changed his opinion more than once. Then, perhaps not unaffected by the mental occlusion of his last days, he began to call the Queen's Colleges "the Godless colleges", a phrase with political appeal in some circles, though some might detect an element of demagoguery in its use. The term had in fact been coined by the Oxford member for Parliament, Sir Robert Inglis, as a Protestant outcry against indifferentism. O'Connell's tone was redolent of his fulminations in 1814 against Cardinal Consalvi as a "perfidious minister" of Pius VII whose negotiations with Viscount Castlereagh would sell out the religion of Ireland; his libelous insinuation that Consalvi had accepted a British bribe of eleven thousand guineas only encouraged the few *zelanti,* or reactionary, cardinals in the Curia, and helped delay Catholic Emancipation until 1829.

We can only speculate whether the Queen's Colleges of Belfast, Cork and Galway would eventually have become Catholic by sheer demographic pressure had the Irish bishops taken advantage of Pope Gregory XVI's hesitancy on the matter. But Dr. Murray's successor, Dr. Cullen, along with Dr. MacHale, the Archbishop of Tuam, did nothing to dissuade the new Pope, Pius IX, from outright condemnation of mixed education. Newman was unclear about what the bishops wanted because the bishops were unclear themselves, even after the Synod of Thurles had condemned the Queen's Colleges in 1850. In a revealing letter in 1868 to his successor as Rector, the future Bishop of Ardagh, Bartholomew Woodlock, Newman would say that he always favored some accommodation with the Peel scheme as practical, if not ideal, hoping for some arrangement along the lines of the new Catholic University of Louvain. As he wrote, Disraeli was considering a full charter for the Dublin institution, and it would certainly exaggerate the case to say that the university failed for want of a charter. Cullen wanted a university in opposition to the Peel scheme, a Catholic univer-

sity for the entire English-speaking world. After twenty-nine
years in Rome—and the hanging of two of his patriot uncles—he
was nervous about the course of Irish nationalism. And at the
same time, though less conspicuously than Dr. MacHale, he did
not imagine a universe large enough to make an Irish university
convincing to anyone outside Ireland. Indeed, the Irish bishops
wanted their university restricted to Irish students. Although
Cullen personally visited Newman in Birmingham in 1851 to
offer the rectorship, Newman came to enjoy the greater confidence of the future Bishop of Kerry, Dr. Moriarty, President of
All Hallows College in Drumcondra, who would come to be
identified with the more liberal faction at the Vatican Council
and who identified himself with the Queen's Colleges party.
And although Newman willingly accepted Cullen's invitation
to deliver a series of discourses at Dublin on the theory of
education as an extended argument against nonsectarian schools,
he understood better than Cullen that the case must be made on
a more philosophical level.

Ireland may have needed Cullen, a politician more than a
philosopher; but politics needs a purpose as philosophy needs a
point, and Cullen was too impetuous for a reasoned purpose.
The Archbishop's neglect of Newman to the point of rudeness,
and his intervention to block a miter for Newman that Wiseman
had already secured for him, are notorious. It seems that Cullen's
obstruction here was not so much ideological, however, as it
was to secure control of the university for himself. Cullen was
not an Irish Manning in any sense of conscious unfriendliness to
Newman, for he lacked Manning's refined skills at calculation,
but Newman does record certain tensions in his retrospective
note of 1872. In 1867, however, when he was delated to Rome
for suspected heresy, he was glad for the Archbishop's decisive
support. Later Newman expressed his gratitude and affection
for Cullen, some of which was the diction of a man whose
life-long inclination was to acknowledge, and sometimes to
invent, the best in people. This could not redeem him in the
eyes of his hosts, who would interrupt their praises of the

Church's universality to accuse Newman of foreignness; and Newman's mind would always be an obstacle to them, for it was not small enough to be measured as great by the small. He wrote privately in 1853 of how Cullen had worn him down after the first two years of their association, during which the prelate had treated him "by silence or abrupt acts". Cardinal Cullen's secretary and nephew, Patrick Moran, by a scrutable providence became a cardinal, but in Australia, where, in 1909, shortly before his death, he defended his uncle's handling of Newman and insisted contrary to fact that Newman had tried to flood the faculty with Englishmen, adding that "it seemed quite repugnant to Irish sentiment that a whole host of English converts should be brought over to a Catholic country to instruct in the paths of learning Irish Catholic youth." The final arrow from his quiver was a summary dismissal of Newman as "a bad Latinist and a poor theologian".[17]

Newman's appreciation of the Irish situation of his day was born precisely of his abiding sense of history. As Cullen was publicly denouncing Fenianism, Newman was more soberly encouraging Eugene O'Curry to recover ancient Celtic manuscripts. The diction of his views on Ireland, which he would argue were not Tudor but Norman, is perhaps matched for balance and expression only by Chesterton, though Newman was less of a democrat and more of an imperialist in the noble sense. For one thing, he shared Cullen's opposition to Repeal, and he once kept a low opinion of O'Connell: "I had an unspeakable aversion to the policy and acts of Mr. O'Connell, because, as I thought, he associated himself with men of all religions and no religion against the Anglican Church, and

---

[17] In W. F. P. Stockley, *Newman, Education and Ireland* (London: Sands and Co., no date), 64–65. Cf. Edmund Campion, *Australian Catholics* (Ringwood, Victoria, 1988), 65. For Newman on Cullen, see the letter to Bartholomew Woodlock (February 23, 1868), in LD XXIV, 40. On O'Connell and Consalvi, see John O'Connell, ed. *The Life and Speeches of Daniel O'Connell M.P.,* vol. II (Dublin, 1846) p. 209; and John Martin Robinson: *Cardinal Consalvi* (New York: St. Martin's Press, 1987), p. 109.

advanced Catholicism by violence and intrigue."[18] But his Tory tone was expansive, and he welcomed a grandson of O'Connell as one of the first twenty students of his university. Later he would upset the neurasthenia of Gerard Manley Hopkins by saying that had he been Irish he would have (in heart) been a rebel. But he added: "To clench the difficulty the Irish character and tastes [are] very different from the English. My fingers will not let me write more."[19] As with Saint John at the end of the Fourth Gospel, one does wish that he might have managed a few more sentences.

Among other intentions, Newman wanted his Dublin lectures to show the Irish that he could be trusted. He succeeded in part. Some of the later criticisms of the way Newman handled the university experiment can sound like attempts to justify the treatment he received in a land proud to have been a nest and refuge of saints and scholars. The faithful poor could not have been more generous. With others it was different. Challenging his own experience and historical erudition, Newman's zeal for the apostolic principle expected nobility in prelates. Moreover, he was puzzled by evidences of a tribalism which thought excellence elitist, individualism disloyal and sensitivity eccentric. Part of the tension has to do, of course, with those simple differences in character and tastes. Newman could be more than a little confused by what Dr. Johnson, in his remark to the Bishop of Killaloe, noticed as a native Irish tendency not to speak well of one another; nor was his reserve at home with the more expansive Celtic habits, which, in spite of outward heartiness, considered forthrightness on significant matters suspect. And in return, the man who measured every word was a curiosity to those for whom quiet on any secondary subject was a mortification.

---

[18] *Apologia pro Vita Sua* (London: Longman, Green and Co., 1890), 223.
[19] Newman to Gerard Manley Hopkins (March 3, 1887), in Ward, 2:527.

Code Words

A long essay of Newman written during the time of his university experiment may well shed some light on his own views of his prospects in Ireland. It certainly provides a useful code for much that he wanted to say but would not say directly at so great a cost of charity. In "The Northmen and Normans in England and Ireland", he goes to lengths to justify an English presence in the other country by an invasion not only justified by Pope Adrian IV for the stated purpose of protecting Christians from internecine disputes but later endorsed by Alexander III and John XXII. The obvious is belabored when it is said, however gracefully, that "an Englishman has no right to open his heart, and indulge his honest affection between him and them." But the "Tudor, not the Plantagenet, introduced the iron age of Ireland", and the reader knows with which house Newman placed himself.

Anyone who objects to what a pope had allowed in Ireland, and the Irish were remarkably free of such criticism, is reminded that, "in matter of fact, the policy which he pursued toward Ireland at the date in question, and which seems at first sight so unfair, is precisely that which he had adopted towards England a century earlier, except that its concomitants in the case of England were far more penal, in severity at least, if not in duration." He speaks, of course, of the Norman Conquest, and what is commonly thought of as an English invasion of Ireland was a Norman invasion inspired by the papal desire to recivilize a land tortured by the Danes, or Northmen. Before the invasion of Henry II from England, some of the Irish princes and chieftains had matched the Danes in their resurgent barbarism: they were Irish themselves who burned the church of Ardbraccan with people in it in 1109, destroyed the monastery of Clonmacnois in 1111, killed the Abbots of Kells, and, on a Sunday too, in 1117, burned Cashel and Lismore in 1121 and plundered Emly two years later, and in 1127 burned the steeple of Trim and those sheltered in it. Newman is not naïvely engaged in self-justification, nor is he loathe to state unpleasant facts: "The wrongs which England has inflicted are faithfully remembered; her services are viewed with incredulity or resentments; her name and fellowship are abominated; the news of her prosperity heard with disgust; the anticipations of her possible reverses nursed and cherished as the best of consolations. The success of France and Russia over her armies, of Yankee or Hindoo, is fervently desired, as the first installment of a debt accumulated through seven centuries. . . . " This was the social psychology he confronted in the university project and is not irrelevant to how he may privately have interpreted the Irish bishops' reaction to his eventual withdrawal from it. It is not that Newman found in Dublin wild men like those of the twelfth century, though he stresses that Dublin was a Danish city, and there is some caution in his diction as he tells it. Nor possibly in his mind had the state of things changed from those distant centuries when "Paris had a gift of civilization at that time which the Irish schools had not."

   To drive the point home, "While we do not doubt that there were far more Irish than English scholars in the eleventh century, we cannot fairly deduce from that superiority that the country priests or peasants of Meath or Leinster had more knowledge of the canons or of the Decalogue than had the clergy and laity of Wessex." One can imagine a certain discomfort in someone like Dr. Cullen reading such passages; and he may have even sensed a delicate barb in the one that ran on: "A saint will influence by his conversation, and preaches by his life; and yet even saints, as we have been showing, are no necessary guarantee of the sanctity of their people. Much less has a school, or college, or seminary, any power to communicate its own attainments or refinement to the neighbourhood in which it is placed." In a line quoted from Lanigan may be a comment on the university trustees with which Newman had to treat: "The Danish clergy of Dublin and the Irish clergy of Armagh were constantly at variance."

   But if these speculations are abstruse, there is something

painfully clarion and declarative, and daring given the situation in which he wrote, when he says something that could apply no less to our time, when old Catholic confidences have grown moribund on the college campuses. The state of Catholic education needs fresh brains and the blood of courage for rescue from idle submission to the spirit of the age, from sacrificing the Catholic principles and becoming clones of secular institutions that have failed their culture. These institutions can be rescued from their moral morass only by the Catholic vision of man and the virtuous intellect. In this code, the "Danes" are the modern Catholic academies that have lost their identity and have grown barbarous to the life of the mind and the virtues; and the "Irish" are the ecclesiastical authorities who either from confused sympathies or insecure wills have allowed this to happen; and the "Normans" are those, we might say, who are sent by the Pope—who really is the Pope—from outside customary careers and upbringing; they may be converts or a new generation of Catholics tired of liberal fatuities, but they intend a Norman invasion for restoring life to a self-destructive and self-betraying intellectual establishment, even if that means on occasion starting new schools as alternatives and models. And it should not surprise us if those inside the decaying academies should complain that the Pope is invading and wrongly trying to dominate from a foreign land: "If, then, the Ostmen, or Danes, of Ireland needed civilizing, and the Irish could not civilize them, and the Normans could, then, for the sake both of the Danes who needed a great benefit, and of the Irish who could not supply it, it was surely not unreasonable in the Pope, nor unsuitable to his high mission, to sanction the expedition of the Normans to Ireland with the object of converting the one and reforming the other."[20]

Newman's academic adventure had put him up against three problem groups. First were the Protestants of the Ascendency,

[20] Newman, *Historical Sketches* (London: Longman, Green and Co., orig. 1856, 1872), 3:307–8; also *passim* 255–312.

whom one convert described as combining "the vulgarity of the English and the brutality of the Irish". And given Newman's tastes, he most likely would have found the former the worse insult.[21] Then there were the bishops: divided among themselves (the Dublin Danes and the Armagh Celts), parochial in their own education and wanting imagination. Most portentous of all was his introduction to a Catholic gentry in Ireland who had so unconsciously aped the Ascendency that their Catholic instincts were disappearing. They were becoming what we would call cultural Catholics. When one of them was told that the Oxford Movement had tried to revive the interior life, fasting and devotions, in England, he answered in surprise: "Well, all that would be totally new in this country."[22] Ireland needed its own Oxford Movement — or Norman Invasion. And soon enough Newman realized that the hard-pressed Irish bishops were asking him to do what they were not doing well themselves.

Thus he faced three challenges that we may have thought were peculiar to our own situation, but these in fact have rarely been absent in the pageant of Catholic education: the tension between ecclesiastical autonomy and state control, the lack of reforming courage on the part of some of the bishops and the subconscious secularism of the young in quest of upward social mobility. At the same time, his attentions were distracted by the Achilli libel trial, the restoration of the English hierarchy and the need to raise funds in a land ravaged by the Great Hunger. As he commuted between England and Ireland for the lectures on the idea of a university, he had other engagements: tracking down young Italian women who had been compromised by the ex-priest and anti-Catholic agitator Achilli, who had had the temerity to sue him, preaching as a phenomenon "The

[21] Anonymous to Newman (December 1851), in Culler, 142.

[22] See Fergal McGrath, S.J., *Newman's University, Ideal and Reality* (London: Longman, Green and Co., 1951), 144. In an untempered moment, Dr. MacHale remarked, "Our high Catholics are rotten to the heart's core, and our middle Catholics are fast corrupting in the same manner, by love of self and place." See W. F. P. Stockley, *Newman, Education and Ireland*, 101–2.

Second Spring" to the restored English bishops, governing the expansion of the Oratory houses and establishing a university. His diaries are edifying to latter-day academics who complain of burnout. Only incidentally does he mention collapsing one day during a regular lecture. And through it all he maintained his usual mortifications and use of the discipline, although these seem to have been the least of his discomforts.

The Irish years are commonly counted as a failure. It is painful to read his university reports, with their sustained hopefulness against odds, dreaming of a university that will attract upward of a hundred Yankees and become the center of English-speaking Catholicism "with Great Britain, Malta (perhaps Turkey or Egypt), and India on one side of it, and North America and Australia on the other." And which, while not yet possessing a museum of antiquities, "has received from the late Msgr. Bettachini . . . a great number of specimens of the birds, amphibia, and recent shells of Ceylon."[23]

The singular success of the medical school shows the importance of a charter, which the university itself lacked, largely because of blatant bigotry in Whitehall: Tory, Liberal and Non-Conformist.[24] But Newman was convinced that, like Louvain, Dublin could do without one. And fairness might ask, if, say, the Armada had won, could there have been in the nineteenth century, or even until these recent years, a Spanish Peel or a Spanish Gladstone providing the rudiments of mixed education in an occupied Britain? The failure to secure a charter notwithstanding, Newman's efforts were a spiritual victory and more, for they have given a philosophical guide by which we can judge ourselves when moral and intellectual neglect of university students is one of the most serious defects of Catholic life in the United States. The very name of Newman having

[23] See *My Campaign in Ireland,* 94 and 182. Cf. *The Idea of a University,* 483ff.

[24] See, for instance, Eugene V. Clark, "Newman and the Catholic University of Ireland", in *Newman Commemorative Essays* (New York: The Paulist Press, 1946), 22.

been surrendered, nondescript religious life programs and pastoral centers are found where once were Newman Centers. The buildings may still be there, but Newman has been taken away. And with him has gone the ability to see that the renewal of education is not a program but, as he called it, a campaign. And by campaign he meant a battle. As the end of education is learning how to think, and as the ultimate end of education is learning to think with the saints, then the battle must be against ignorance and falsehood. He writes at the beginning of his struggle: "The battle there will be what it was in Oxford twenty years ago", and such men as Keble and Pusey, "who have been able to do so little against Liberalism in Oxford will be renewing the fight although not in their persons in Ireland".[25] However much some of the bishops who had invited him to Ireland may have cautiously admired him, they had not a clue to what he meant.

A Brief against the Trashing of Culture

If we think Newman prophetic in measuring the residue content of the liberalism in his day, then we may also presume to confess this with him: vindication of the idea of a university will not come on the campuses by bureaucratic compromise and moral innocuousness but by genius and holiness. Divine Wisdom has been ever generous in providing these to the Church, and human wisdom consists in cultivating them as one. Newman's idea was ancient, and not ancient because it was aged but because it was true. Thus it was as new as it is old; but from the cultural isolation of modern education, the idea seems only archaic and novel. It will stay limp like that until the Church's universities make bold to say that an idea can be not only agreeable but true. And Catholic leaders will recover their prophetic mantle when they publicly denounce those who

[25] Newman to Mrs. Froude (October 1851), in Ward, 1:312.

rant, as they did a few years ago at Stanford with politicians like Mr. Jesse Jackson, weaving among the students, "Hey, hey, ho, ho! Western culture's got to go!"

Newman's distaste for the institution of gentleman commoners at Oxford who were not obliged to serious pursuits, his fund-raising for needy students and his novel provision for night classes for young working men should purge the charge that Newman meant to foster unjust privilege by his concept of the university as a place for gentlemen.[26] His aim was against mere vocational education as it was promoted by the utilitarians at the University of London in 1827. Shallow populism, which has made modern American education little more than job training at the expense of cultural literacy, takes its moral tincture from a middle-class refinement of the naturalist assumptions of the Enlightenment. For Newman, it was a most vicious threat to classical liberal learning, which is meant to "free" the mind. This, after all, is the etymology of the "liberal" in liberal arts, and utilitarian liberalism was the blatant contradiction of classical liberalism. Education is half itself in teaching how to make a living; it is all it should be when it teaches how to make a life. The inarticulateness of the new jargon phrase, "Get a life", is a poignant appeal for what Newman meant from a generation deprived of what Newman meant.

Recent best-selling criticisms of our system have recognized this, but for the most part they do not accept or even acknowledge Newman's solution. Allan Bloom, for example, will speak in *The Closing of the American Mind* of virtue but not of grace, because his sympathies are rooted in the prejudices of Rousseau, whom he would make the father of modern humanities, and of Kant, whom he even calls "a significant natural scientist".[27]

---

[26] See *The Idea of a University,* x, xi, xvi. Also *My Campaign in Ireland,* 47–48, 52–53, 128. Students in his own household at No. 6 Harcourt Street included a French vicomte, an Irish baronet, two sons of a French prince and a Polish count; these were witnesses to their confidence in him more than his confidence in them.

[27] Alan Bloom, *The Closing of the American Mind* (New York: Simon

He simply cannot understand the ordering of grace upon nature as Newman has it. When Bloom says the only method of reform is "the good old Great Books approach", he is arguing for the eighteenth-century gentleman by whose urbanity "vice lost half its evil by losing all its grossness." Newman seems to have had that line from Burke's *Reflections on the Revolution in France* echoing in his mind in 1850 when he delivered the second of his lectures on *Anglican Difficulties,* for there he damns with faint praise Anglicanism's ability "to deprive vice of its grossness". By the time of his university lectures, he has developed this irony into an indictment: when this religion of philosophy "is strong enough to have a will of its own, and is lifted up with an idea of its own importance, and attempts to form a theory, and to lay down a principle, and to carry out a system of ethics, and undertakes the moral education of the man, then it does but abet the evils to which at first it seemed instinctively opposed."[28] If left unchecked, it produces the mentality that thinks all religions are superstitions and considers an M.B.A. a scholarly degree.

In 1987, various English-speaking countries proposed that the

---

and Schuster, 1987), 349 and 35–59. With his encomium of Kant, Bloom served evidence of a hardly ever noticed facet of the closing of the American *academic* mind. It systematically disregards, as a habit of the academic "establishment", scholarly works that discredit its hallowed clichés about cultural history. A classic illustration of this is Bloom's failure to refer to the devastating exposure of Kant's shocking incompetence in matters scientific as revealed in chapter 8 of Stanley L. Jaki's Gifford Lectures, *The Road of Science and the Ways to God,* a book published in 1978 and republished twice as a paperback by the University of Chicago Press, Bloom's own home turf. Established academic circles have also ignored Jaki's translation of Kant's cosmogony, *Universal Natural History and Theory of the Heavens* (Edinburgh: Scottish Academic Press, 1981). No wonder. There a hundred-page-long introduction and about as many pages of notes place Kant in the context of a meticulously researched history of astronomy and cosmology during the eighteenth century, with the result that Kant appears for what he really was with respect to science—a rank amateur.

[28] *The Idea of a University,* 202. Cf. ibid., preface, xvi, and Bloom, 344.

Congregation for Catholic Education use *The Idea of a University* when revising its draft schema for a pontifical document on Catholic universities.[29] Although Bloom was writing for a far different purpose, his failure to mention Newman once in his entire critique of liberal education is a thundering lacuna, but it is not a surprise. Nor is it surprising that Newman was ignored in Wisconsin at the Land O'Lakes Conference of Catholic Educators that produced on July 23, 1967, a prescription for Bloom's kind of scholar. It was signed by dozens of presidents of Catholic colleges and universities, met little censure from the official teachers of the Church and played no little role in the consequent decay of Catholic higher education. Indeed, some of the signatories received preferment. Like the Oxford Protestantism of the 1830s, neither the Bloom book nor the Wisconsin statement has been "susceptible of so high a temper" as an authentic campaign for academic reform requires.[30] In some universities, students who have paid over $100,000 for their four years receive Latin diplomas telling them that they are Bachelors of Arts, and with the document is included a slip of paper with a translation of the words. A call for higher standards will not improve this. Remedy requires some redress of the old nominalism that launched the whole disorder. The closing of the American mind will not be cured by the opening of the American mind but by the strengthening of the American mind. And this means redirecting attention from the line of values to the line of the good. And only Catholicism is an infallible guide. Otherwise, universities will continue to disintegrate into detached "departments" unable to speak a common language of civilization. The medical will suspect the motives of the law faculty, and both will think that the philosophy faculty is a repository for relaxed minds. Then the University should be named a Schizophrenia, for it will be a place for separating mental science.

---

[29] Congregation for Catholic Education, "Summary Responses to Draft Schema of Catholic Universities", in *Origins* 17 (March 24, 1988): 699.

[30] Newman to Mrs. Froude, in Ward, 1:312.

The Degeneracy of the Land O'Lakes Statement

As early as the Tamworth Reading Room letters, Newman was certain that even a classical education based on other than Christianity as its element and principle would degenerate into either "a mawkish, frivolous and fastidious sentimentalism" or "a dry, unamiable longheadedness" or "an uppish, supercilious temper, much inclined to scepticism".[31] The Land O'Lakes "Statement on the Nature of the Contemporary Catholic University" succumbed to all three, expressing itself incidentally in an English as bereft of the standards Newman enjoyed as it is of his logic. It already sounds dated as Newman's *Idea* cannot be, trapped in a 1960s time warp, the abject proof that thought must surrender to the slavery of contemporaneity when it is not "formed" by the liberating disciplines of the arts.

Certainly with the best intentions, a prominent churchman, not unrepresentative of the Land O'Lakes school of thought, upset the economy of Newman's intelligence of obedience when he said in a 1986 commencement address at Notre Dame: "Theology will also enrich the Church if it takes into account the teaching office of the bishops and the Pope, not slavishly but with honorable fidelity."[32] Unlike Newman, he is not careful to define his terms, but he does imply that there are theologians who might enslave themselves to the Magisterium. A servile theologian would be a contradiction as Newman understands theological science. The teaching office of the Church precludes unthinking obedience precisely by the fact

---

[31] *Discussions and Arguments on Various Subjects* (London: Longman, Green and Co., 1918), 275. Cf. *The Idea of a University,* where he speaks in the sixth discourse (145) of "a generation frivolous, narrow-minded, and resourceless".

[32] Bishop James Malone, Commencement Address at the University of Notre Dame, May 18, 1986, in *Origins* 15:117. In contrast, the Second Vatican Council speaks of religious assent as the "religious submission of mind and will". *Lumen Gentium,* no. 25. Cf. *Dei Verbum,* no. 5, and the First Vatican Council, *De Fide,* Dens. no. 1789 (no. 3008).

that it teaches essentially as the seat of authority only because it is integrally the seat of wisdom. The commencement speaker made the same dialectical *faux pas* that led Berengar of Tours astray in his exaggerated rejection of scholastic priorities in the eleventh century. No one in the audience, not even all those new bachelors of arts, seemed to have detected this. Not even after four years in a midwestern Catholic university. Perhaps the day was too sultry. Or perhaps the microphone had failed, or the distractions of so exciting an occasion did not encourage serious allusions. Or perhaps, even in a Catholic university, they had not been told about Berengar of Tours.

Servile conformity is the mark of a mind that has not enjoyed the philosophical completeness of liberal learning, which is the propaedeutic for theology and all science. About nine hundred years ago, such had been the trespass of Abelard, who, one will remember, was one of the patrons of the fictitious "British and Foreign Truth Society" satirized in Newman's *Loss and Gain* for having discovered that truth cannot be found. Abelard's own biography makes for more than a little commentary on the present moral state of the Catholic schools; his neglect of the liberal arts for the new philosophy cast him into a downward spiral of rebellion, impurity and, finally, heresy. Here is a mediaeval anticipation of the Kantian antinomies to which I have alluded and which pops its head up whenever one speaks of a dialectic between slavish obedience to religion and honorable fidelity.

Intellectualism so partisan may be the romance of the natural man and even the reverie of the pagan gentleman, but it is not the logic of the Catholic scholar. Liberal education untutored by ecclesial obedience has a tendency to turn into "pick and choose" intellectualism. Says Newman, "This Intellectualism first and chiefly comes into collisions with precept, then with doctrine, then with the very principle of dogmatism;—a perception of the Beautiful becomes the substitute for faith . . . even within the pale of the Church, and with the most unqualified profession of her Creed, it acts, if left to itself, as an element of corruption and infidelity." With grave prophecy, Newman warned that a university captive to such corruption would become a religion of its own, an institutional rival to the Church.[33]

The commencement speaker to whom I have referred remarked how, after several decades, "the Catholic community no longer lives at the edge of the society." Now, Newman spoke of the condition in Ireland, where Catholics had for centuries been deprived of their "legitimate stations, duties, employments"; and yet he explained with probity why his *desideratum* was not "the manners and habits of gentlemen", as such upward social mobility is the aim of utilitarianism but not of Catholic education. Newman's description of the gentleman who was not "formed" is the closest we can find to the profile of what the nominally Catholic universities seem content to manufacture, the deontologized *arriviste* commonly called a Yuppie:

> Mistaking animal spirits for vigour, and over-confident in their health, ignorant of what they can bear and how to manage themselves, they are immoderate and extravagant; and fall into sharp sicknesses. This is an emblem of their minds; at first they have no principles laid within them as a foundation for the intellect to build upon; they have no discriminating convictions, and no grasp of consequences. And therefore they talk at random, if they talk much, and cannot help being flippant, or what is emphatically called *young.* They are merely dazzled by phenomena instead of perceiving things as they are.[34]

The Land O'Lakes statement begins: "The Catholic University today must be a university in the full modern sense of the word."[35] With so portentous a start, one wants an explanation

---

[33] *The Idea of a University,* 218.

[34] Ibid., preface, xvi–xvii.

[35] "Statement on the Nature of the Contemporary Catholic University", Land O'Lakes, Wisconsin (July 23, 1967), sec. 1; cf. sec. 9. The definition of a university reappears in sec. 5 of "The Contemporary Catholic University", a position paper prepared by the North American section of the Interna-

of what the full modern sense of the word might be, and one is also stimulated by the confidence of the declaration to ask why the university "must" conform to it. "Is must", asked Elizabeth I, "a word to be used to princes?" There is no definition and no account of the obligation to conform to an age that has failed in its experiments to disprove the truths of God. Jealousy for its autonomy has submitted the Catholic university to the senile dictates of a dying social liberalism. But having squeezed themselves into the tight harness of contemporaneity, the signatories of the mercifully brief Land O'Lakes text fall into the three types Newman predicted. The mawkish rhapsodize about "warm personal dialogue"; the longheaded diagram "a self-developing and self-deepening society of students and faculty in which the consequences of Christian truth are taken seriously in person-to-person relationships"; the superciliously inclined to scepticism proclaim that "the Catholic university must have a true autonomy and academic freedom in the face of authority of whatever kind, lay or clerical, external to the academic community itself."[36]

But Newman has insisted that the Catholicity of a university

---

tional Federation of Catholic Universities in *Notre Dame Report* 1971–1972 (South Bend, Ind.: University of Notre Dame, 1972), 103ff. Its appendix (111) includes the statement: "[The Catholic University] is an independent organization serving Christian purposes but not subject to ecclesiastical-juridical control, censorship or supervision." But in 1993, the encyclical *Veritatis Splendor,* no. 116 would teach: "A particular responsibility is incumbent upon bishops with regard to Catholic institutions. Whether these are agencies for the pastoral care of the family or for social work, or institutions dedicated to teaching or health care, bishops can canonically erect and recognize these structures and delegate certain responsibilities to them. Nevertheless, bishops are never relieved of their own personal obligations. It falls to them, in communion with the Holy See, both to grant the title 'Catholic' to Church-related schools, universities, health care facilities and counselling services, and, in cases of a serious failure to live up to that title, to take it away."

[36] "Statement on the Nature of the Contemporary Catholic University", sec. 1.

is secured by more than teaching theology as a branch of knowledge: "Hence a direct and active jurisdiction of the Church over it and in it is necessary, lest it should become the rival of the Church with the community at large in those theological matters which to the Church are exclusively committed, — acting as the representative of the intellect, as the Church is the representative of the religious principle." Little direct respect for this principle seems to have embued the hierarchy, however. One cardinal, in support of the Land O'Lakes ethos, has recommended a nondirective approach to keeping universities Catholic and cited his practice of annual luncheons with college presidents as a means of doing this; in the same address he said that the secular model for Catholic higher education is irreversible and that in ordinary practice the bishop should not interfere with those engaged in the daily operation of the schools. Not to belabor the analogy, again we have here an example of the Neville Chamberlain confidence in dialogue and an underestimation of the gravity of the issue.[37]

The sentimentality of the Wisconsin document is the etiquette of an undisciplined mind and is precisely what Newman campaigned against in both Oriel College and Dublin. To wear one's heart on one's sleeve means that it has been disconnected from the mind. This happened to the dislocated moral interiority of Kant, and so he quivered all his days between idealism and empiricism. The Land O'Lakes "Idea O' a University" does the same, groping for a false independence by an unthinking acceptance of the Kantian antinomies of will and reason. An unconscious Kantian denial of active agency to the material world may have led the signatories to assume that obedience to the historical fact of the Church compromises academic freedom. And what is this distrust of a *cultus externus* but an anemic

---

[37] *The Idea of a University*, 215. Cf. also the remarks of Joseph Cardinal Bernardin at Fordham University, in George Kelly, *Catholic Higher Education: Is It in or out of the Church?* (Front Royal, Va.: Christendom Press, 1992), 30–32.

version of the diatribes in the fourth book of Kant's *Religion within the Limits of Reason Alone?* They would not understand Newman's profession of faith according to the formulary of Pius IV. They do not consider the prior claim of the freedom of the Church in relation to the university, and of the freedom of the university in relation to its members, and ultimately of natural religion in relation to interior moral receptivity. Their statement materially departs from the teaching of the Second Vatican Council, which is reiterated in the revised Code of Canon Law.

Cardinal Newman was an "absent Father" of the Second Vatican Council in no issue more than in his defense of the freedom of the Church to teach. To tailor this freedom to one's personal measurement is to be like the liberal gentleman who is "merciful to the absurd". Newman would hardly have been satisfied with that Council's pallid exposition of a philosophy of Catholic education. It could have said more, and indeed its preparatory documents said much more, but the intervention of American bishops removed numerous exhortations and specifics from the declaration *Gravissimum Educationis.* Its promulgation in 1965 promised documents to firm it up, thus satisfying other Council Fathers who wanted to defeat it because of its generalities. It took twenty-five years for the apostolic constitution *Ex Corde Ecclesiae* to appear with a classical definition of academic freedom as "free search for the whole truth about nature, man, and God" consistent with a theology that is "faithful to scripture, tradition, and the Church's magisterium". But several years earlier, in 1987, at a conference at De Paul University, the presidents of universities including Notre Dame, Fordham and the Catholic University of America itself had conjured up again the bewitching spirit of Land O'Lakes to locate the "Catholic" identity of such institutions in "continuing inspiration" and "well-attended liturgies", with no philosophical definition such as Newman or the Magisterium would recognize.[38]

[38] Cf. Canons 808, 810, 812; *Ex Corde Ecclesiae,* I, nos. 4, 7, 12, 13, 17, 20;

Personal Influence and Universal Knowledge

The statutes of the Catholic University of Ireland were modeled on the revived University of Louvain, then less than twenty years old. But Newman's experience was of the Oxford collegiate system. Even in its most degenerate period in the late eighteenth century, it had provided a means of personal influence necessary if the university was to be of moral consequence. Newman sided more with Edward Copleston's moderate reforming ambition than with Pusey's bias for the tutorial arrangement. His thesis as it develops more in the Essays than in the Discourses is plain enough: the university is the province of the professorial system entrusted with the essential being of the institution, and the college is the province of the tutorial system charged with its integral well-being. The university is "a place of teaching universal knowledge", but colleges and halls of residence are the instruments that the Church uses to manifest the good of the Faith.[39] The Land O'Lakes statement, in contrast, assumes that the university and the college are totally distinct according

---

American Catholic Higher Education: Essential Documents, 280–81. Conference on Catholic Higher Education (April 30–May 1, 1987): in *Newsletter of the Fellowship of Catholic Scholars,* September 1987. For the history of *Gravissimum Educationis,* see *American Participation in the Second Vatican Council,* ed. Vincent Yzermans (N.Y.: Sheed and Ward, 1967), 543–65.

[39] The subject is discussed at length in *Historical Sketches,* vol. 3, chaps. 15 and 19. "If I were to describe as briefly and popularly as I could, what a University was, I should draw my answer from its ancient designation of a *Studium Generale,* or 'School of Universal Learning'" (ibid., chap. 2, p. 6). Cf. Newman's tribute to Copleston in *The Idea of a University,* 157. The Newman Movement began as an attempt to adapt Newman's vision to the American university structure. Following an experiment at the University of Pennsylvania, the first "Newman Club" was organized by Timothy L. Harrington at the University of Pennsylvania in the early 1890s. Cf. John Whitney Evans, *The Newman Movement* (South Bend, Ind.: University of Notre Dame Press, 1980), 19ff.

to the common American model and treats them as such. Historically in the American scheme, a college has been dedicated chiefly to the formation of undergraduates in the liberal arts, although recent grandiose tendencies to rename many colleges universities has only inflated the currency and, as Sir William Gilbert would have it, "When every one is somebodee/ Then no one's anybody." Newman only wanted a university in the mediaeval sense, that is, one that "merely brought a number of young men together for three or four years and then sent them away", in contrast to an institution that "gave degrees to any person who passed an examination in a wide range of subjects".[40] The striving of the late-twentieth-century Catholic university to be like the latter is considered by many to be progressive, especially if public funds are among the trophies. Such money may build libraries and regild domes, but in the end it will be used to buy a potter's field. There is, for example, one venerable Catholic institution that has lost sight of its saints and has a law building once named "St. Thomas More" now known as "More" and whose new library is named for a congressman.

Newman does not disallow polytechnic study; he founded an engineering school and bought a medical school. But he reserves such to the academy, according to the French and English arrangement. The doctoral system as it is generally known in the United States is of German design, which took shape after the cultural trauma of Prussian defeat at the Battle of Jena in 1806. Philosophically formed from Kantian and Fichtean subjectivism, with its deference to social evolution, it gradually came to invest scientific research with the prestige formerly reserved to the classical arts. Only a decade after Newman's

[40] *The Idea of a University*, 145. Here, when he says a university is "not a foundry, or a mint, or a treadmill", he echoes the scornful reference to the University of London as "Gower Street College" in *Discussions and Arguments*, 274. He would certainly say the same of today's size-conscious Catholic institutions. See n. 11 supra.

Dublin project, the Johns Hopkins University introduced the German type to the United States, and Johns Hopkins is where Woodrow Wilson went for his doctorate when he had exhausted the scientific resources of Princeton. The widespread doctorate remained rather foreign to the English system until well into this century; and even in the United States the total number of Ph.D.'s granted by all universities and eighty-two independent professional schools as late as 1920 was 532. Now Wilson was the first president to have earned a doctorate; but you need only to match his monographs on historical philosophy with Theodore Roosevelt's essay on "History as Literature" to wish that Wilson had not so confined his parson's soul to the advanced academy. Roosevelt seems so much more the complete man, and when he did address the faculty of the Sorbonne, his hearty decibels in favor of virtue and life's adventure were ever more convincing than anything Wilson was capable of in his Fourteen Points. As personalities, Newman's educated man might have found a day with Roosevelt more trying than one with Wilson, but he would have preferred to be with Roosevelt for an eternity.

Newman foresaw that, without the obedience of faith, the aesthetic intellectualism of the German system gradually would divinize experience, dehistoricize culture and isolate judgment by bonding it to the tyranny of immediacy. The result would be a miscellaneous erudition that could not withstand moral fragmentation. A university is not Catholic, then, that has no unified objective guide for its scientific inventiveness or that countenances moral choices as alternatives to the natural law.

The Land O'Lakes statement describes a university "where the students can learn by personal experience to consecrate their talent and learning to worthy social purposes". But what are talent and learning? Recent surveys indicate little that would have impressed Newman. In his seventh discourse, Newman says, "The University, if it refuses the foremost place to professional interests, does but postpone them to the formation of the citizen."[41] Surely he means something more demanding and salutary than the consecration of a scattering of information. His secret is public: he means the ideal of the free citizen according to the structure of *paedeia,* which, if a vague notion to twentieth-century educators meeting in a pleasant Wisconsin retreat, was as alive to Newman in nineteenth-century Ireland as it was to the Sophists in Greece twenty-five hundred years ago. The concept is of education as initiation into a culture. Protestantism could not secure it by its tendency to sentimentalism, and liberalism could not realize it by its obligations to Gnosticism. Catholic modernism, rife at Land O'Lakes, combined the two mental infirmities.

The Gnostic Fantasy

In the third century, Plotinus had astutely located the rejection of *paedeia* at the core of Gnostic alienation. His point is germane to Newman's claim that only Catholic Christianity has the ability to preserve the perduring truths of culture against dehumanizing influences. Newman's salute to the Irish saints and scholars is no less a salute to the Periclean ideal of the free man, the figure whose ability to reason saves him from the dictate of the cliché. And high among today's clichés is the belief that pluralism has replaced a unifying culture. "Hey, hey, ho, ho, Western culture's got to go!" If great, dead, white European males are dismissed as archetypes because they are dead, white European males, there is little chance that minds will concern themselves with a male Jew dead on a Middle Eastern cross. "Hey, hey, ho, ho" is the vulgarians' assault on *paedeia.* For *paedeia* is not conformity of thought but uniformity of conviction that there is such a thing as thought. The

---

[41] Ibid., 167. Thus in *My Campaign in Ireland* (249) he faults the notion of a university that is "a sort of bazaar or hotel, where everything is showy, self-sufficient and changeable".

invocation of plural values over against the fact of culture surrenders thought to feeling. *Paedeia* was vital to the ancient Gael, as it was to Saint Augustine, who did not think doctrine limited the freedom of cultured man, for it secured it; in contrast, the Gnostic distrust of Providence and its misinformed anthropology were unspoken prompters to the utilitarian lethargy of the mind. The utilitarian is ever at heart a nominalist, and the nominalist's subliminal fantasy is the brooding vapor of Gnosticism.

The educational theory in the Land O'Lakes statement is tinged with the same sort of deracinated Gnostic impulse. One evidence is its call for liturgical experimentation, certainly a misplaced function in the university. The chaos that followed, no less than the moral disarray on the campuses, continues to be an unhappy ritualization of cultural amnesia. "Hey, hey, ho, ho! First the ritual language has got to go! Then the man at the altar has got to go! Then the altar has got to go!" In the words of Plotinus against the Gnostics, even the least imaginative can detect the words of Newman after reading the Land O'Lakes statement:

> We are not told what virtue is or under what different kinds it appears . . . we do not learn what constitutes it or how it is acquired, how the Soul is tended, how it is cleansed. For to say "Look to God" is not helpful without some instruction as to what this looking imports: it might very well be said that one can "look" and still sacrifice no pleasure, still be the slave of impulse, repeating the word "God" but held in the grip of every passion and making no effort to master any.[42]

---

[42] Plotinus, *Enneads,* II, ix, 15, trans. S. MacKenna, rev. ed. (London, 1969), 147–48. Cf. A. Louth, *Discerning the Mystery* (Oxford: Clarendon Press, 1983), 75–77. See also W. Jaeger, *Paedeia: The Ideals of Greek Culture* (Oxford: University Press, 1939).

Freedom from Infidelity

The 1967 conference came at a time marked by concerns that occupied Newman in the 1850s: the temptation of mixed education, an imprecision of episcopal guidance and a utilitarian bias in the middle class. Where Newman chose a Catholic course, the 1967 signatories succumbed to the imperative of the "infidelity of the day". The conference set the agenda for an entire generation's pedagogy; and, like Friar Bacon's retreat from Aristotle's realism, it has ended up *"operose nihil agendo"*. The Land O'Lakes Conference was to the Catholic universities what the Yalta Conference was to Eastern Europe. In the encyclical *Centesimus Annus,* the Pope cited Yalta by corrosive innuendo as one of those historical examples of how calculating irresponsibility exacts a toll beyond calculation: "It seemed that the European order resulting from the Second World War and sanctioned by the *Yalta Agreements* could only be overturned by another war. Instead, it has been overcome by the non-violent commitment of people who, while always refusing to yield to the force of power, succeeded time after time in finding effective ways of bearing witness to the truth."[43] However capable the actors may have been, whatever their moral rectitude, whoever was their inspiring voice, Yalta remains a painful picture of that principle no less real for its frequent repeating: weakness has done more harm than vice. And as that has been so in the affairs of men, it has been so in the highest affairs of men as they have been lived in the Church. Few who know the name Yalta will recognize the much different and far-removed place called Land O'Lakes. If they think the comparison is extreme, however, they will not think so when they have lived long enough in a culture shaped by a population whose education did not shape them, or misshaped them, and let them loose to influence a world through a nation whose strength determines much in the world.

[43] *Centesimus Annus,* no. 23.

As the Church tries to recover the economy of integrity and essence in the institution, there will be new critics, as Newman had his. And the Benthamites will honor the Church's champions no more than they honored Newman in his most vital years. But Newman understood such neglect as its own tribute. A society corrupted by its self-interests, and exhausting its capacities on maintaining those interests, will have no good word for Catholic truth and will decorate Catholic educators with honors only when they have become the slaves of Athens and not its free citizens. When even Newman would have expressed some things in a way Pius IX chose not to, and so for instance labored over his fifth discourse on "Knowledge Its Own End" to explain that detached philosophical pursuits are not contrary to the dogmatic principle, he knew that the idea of a university was not his but the sagacity of an apostle. He was no slave to that authority because he had been freed by it:

In the midst of our difficulties I have one ground of hope, just one stay, which supports me if I begin to despond, and to which I have ever come round when the question of the possible and the expedient is brought into discussion. It is the decision of the Holy See; St. Peter has spoken, it is he who has enjoined that which seems to us so unpromising. He has spoken, and has a claim on us to trust him. He is no recluse, no solitary student, no dreamer about the past, no doter upon the dead and gone, no projector of the visionary. He for eighteen hundred years has lived in the world; he has seen all fortunes, he has encountered all adversaries, he has shaped himself for all emergencies. If ever there was a power on earth who had an eye for the times, who has confined himself to the practicable, and has been happy in his anticipations, whose words have been facts, and whose commands prophecies, such is he in the history of the ages, who sits from generation to generation in the Chair of the Apostles, as the Vicar of Christ, and the Doctor of His Church.[44]

---

[44] *The Idea of a University*, 13. For a study of the fifth discourse and the brief of Pius IX, see McGrath, 273ff.

VII

CHESTERTON AND THE MEDIA

A Man with a Message

The media *philosophe* Marshall McLuhan converted to Catholicism after reading *What's Wrong with the World,* by G. K. Chesterton (1874–1936). The same McLuhan was a consultant to the Second Vatican Council, admittedly on the infrequently cited Decree on the Means of Social Communication, *Inter Mirifica.* Given the liturgical dereliction all around, one of his warnings is crushingly poignant: that the use of microphones on the altar would destroy the psychology of the Latin rite, for it would signal the replacement of sacral prayer with pedagogic conversation. But to our immediate purpose: if McLuhan's dictum holds true, that the medium is the message, Chesterton proved it. For all he wrote and spoke was what he was, more than what he thought or felt. He clothed himself in letters, but he was the message; and that is why getting the message across was a vocation for him when for many others it was but a profession, and it was a vocation because it was part of a romance that breaks the hypnotic slumber of pedants.

You have to observe Chesterton as a fact; he cannot be taken apart as a theory. When a man is taken apart, he quickly ceases to be alive; and there is a proprietary form of criticism that is very like vivisection. Cain slew Abel; so far as we know, he did not compound his crime by drawing and quartering him. But Chesterton is very much alive—no thanks to the universities who neglected him for so long that he became a lacuna to young minds. It has been estimated that no English writer is quoted as frequently now, save for Shakespeare. A quotable Chesterton on any subject is like a splashable ocean; he cannot be undone by being quoted. It is just hard to know where to begin and end. But not to begin anywhere is endless snobbery.

As he wrote in *The Illustrated London News* for December 16, 1905:

> The uneducated are, by their nature, the real conservers of the past; because they are the people who are really not interested in beauty, but interested in interest. The poor have this advantage over the cultivated class, that the poor (like a few of the best of the very rich) are not affected by the fashions: they keep things because they are quaint or out of the current line of thought. They keep Old Masters because they are old, not because they have recently been "discovered". They preserve old fashions until the time when they shall become new fashions. For the man who is ten years behind his time is always ten years nearer to the return of that time.

For thirty-one years, beginning in 1905, Chesterton wrote weekly columns of about two thousand words which were read widely in the English-speaking world. Against the background of nearly a hundred books and plays and collections of poetry, he continued this outpouring of 1,535 columns for *The Illustrated London News,* whose editors required that he declare early on (April 7, 1906) the constraints of his contract: "I am not allowed in these columns to discuss politics or religion, which is inconvenient as they are the only two subjects which seem to me to have the slightest element of interest for a sane man." He remained sane and flaunted mental balance by writing about the great euphemism for politics and religion: that is, he wrote about the world. The columns in fact supported some of the century's most astute political and theological discourse.

His subject, addressed in a thousand ways under a thousand titles, was the soul and body; every declaration he could muster doomed the idealist dogma of man as mind and mind alone. That conceit to him was vulgar; and it was the definitive vulgarity. But nothing could be farther from his vision of the true man than a crusade to protect the Chesterton literature from what is more vulgarly called vulgarization. You might as well object to the Vulgate. With close to moral certainty we may say that Chesterton esteemed the Vulgate as the book of great common speech with the same passion he would have hurled against the *haute vulgarisation* of the New American Bible. His feet were firmly planted against the condescending snob whose commitments to flat impressions overwhelmed commitments to the romance of creation.

His wife, Frances, revealed her own literary prudence when she chose lines from Walter de la Mare for his memorial card:

> Knight of the Holy Ghost, he goes his way
> Wisdom his motley, Truth his loving jest;
> The mills of Satan keep his lance in play,
> Pity and innocence his heart at rest.

But does this describe the best-known contemporary journalists and news reporters? Can it be said in the best of spirits that columnists in *The New York Times* are knights of the Holy Ghost or of anyone? Do the television news analysts wear wisdom as motley and make truth their loving jest? Do the mills of Satan keep even the lances of MacNeil and Lehrer at play? Do pity and innocence perceptibly animate the hearts of Dan Rather and Sam Donaldson? I only propose the question, without passing judgment. It may be that sometimes the answer is yes. In such instances it would be remarkable, while in the case of Chesterton it could not have been otherwise.

Even Evelyn Waugh, trying to find something dismissive about him, said that he was a lovable and much-loved man abounding in charity and humility, and these do not usually make for greatness in art.[1] But in Chesterton's case, this charity and humility were the highest product of the arts of communication; for he used himself to show people that they are better than they realize because they are offered a divinely endowed potential for realizing how ridiculous they can be. It is the essential function of the media to do this, and it is the one

---

[1] In William F. Buckley, Jr., *Right Reason* (New York: Doubleday, 1985), 346.

thing the media never seem to do, at least they never seem to do it intentionally. Which is why its scions fail in pity and innocence. They have altered knighthood, and their nightly news is not Chesterton's knightly news.

An almost unsettling trait in Chesterton is the farsightedness that needed no pince-nez. Before television, he saw it coming. Of course he was a champion of deregulation, and this is what he says of the BBC in anticipation of contemporary media monopolies: "Suppose you had told some of the old Whigs, let alone Liberals, that there was an entirely new type of printing press, eclipsing all others; and that as this was to be given to the King, all printing would henceforth be government printing. They would be roaring like rebels, or even regicides, yet that is exactly what we have done with the whole new invention of the wireless."[2]

From all accounts, he surprised himself with the discovery that he had become something of a radio celebrity. It began with a series of talks that the BBC invited him to begin in 1932, following his broadcast to the United States on Christmas Day, 1931, when he had declared that Christmas was no more old-fashioned than the wireless. He seemed to find it hard to imagine how indeed he had become part of the message. And significantly, the celebrity added upon his well-established literary reputation came through the broadcast medium; not being visible, he seemed to blend with the words as he had already done on a more restricted scale in his books. His lectures and debates, while amusing and often brilliant, were not of this order, and, I suspect, it was because the figure got in the way of the man.

Frances Chesterton understood the mystique of "image" better than he, and early in his career she crafted the romantic, if not exotic, outfit that became his signature. It was hardly necessary and even became a distraction. Frances could have been a useful media consultant to some later presidential candi-

[2] Maisie Ward, *Gilbert Keith Chesterton* (New York: Sheed and Ward, 1943), 630.

dates in America, but creating a persona for G.K. was like petrifying Mount Rushmore. And yet it is this very preoccupation with the perceived self that has become so detrimental in today's media. It is bad enough in the literary posing of syndicated columnists; it is worse with the celebrity newscasters; and it reaches new depths when journalists become television fixtures. A passage from *The Incredulity of Father Brown*, which most certainly is based on his own experience when his ship docked in New York in 1921, places Chesterton in close sympathy with public figures victimized by a self-important press: "America has a genius for the encouragement of fame . . . and he found himself held up on the quay by a group of journalists, as by a gang of brigands, who asked him questions about all the subjects on which he was least likely to regard himself as an authority. . . ."[3]

The Solemn Duty

He did say, it is true, that "writing badly is the definition of journalism."[4] But the journalism of his day expected a quality far superior to what passes now. It took far more seriously the life of the mind. He was patient with the obtuseness of hired intelligence as it was beginning to make universities the monopoly of polemicists both idealist and materialist; but when he considered creative thought, as Coleridge described the domain of integral imagination, he anticipated its present tendency to nest everywhere but in the academic nest, and he did not underestimate the ability of professors to sit on eggs not their own. The formal study of English was a novelty in the university curriculum; previously it had been the domain of those who wrote English. The journalist of Chesterton's vintage was

[3] G. K. Chesterton, *The Incredulity of Father Brown* (New York: Dodd, Mead, 1926), 25–26.
[4] G. K. Chesterton, *A Handful of Authors: Essays on Books and Writers* (New York: Sheed and Ward, 1953), 202.

still a man of letters, though he was possibly the last and brightest of the breed: E. V. Lucas spun out the definitive life of Charles Lamb, and J. L. Hammond wrote his economic history, as newspaper men. Today it would be like Walter Cronkite editing the monographs of Montesquieu. We do not expect our journalists to be noble writers; and as for television commentators, we are content when they show an ability to read. As Dr. Johnson said about women preaching, the fact that it is not done well would be overwhelmed by a general astonishment at its being done at all.

Yet what makes the distinction between someone like him and some of today's media figures, who by comparison are like lint, is Chesterton's subordination of the self to a truth. This was far more significant than the breadth of his knowledge. He was more than a Renaissance man; his reference is positively deep, and deep enough to dig beneath anything so occasional as a renaissance until he strikes the radical birth of order and truth. It is a gift for making obvious the obvious through parallelism, what Belloc called "the illustration of a truth already known and perceived". The imaginative faculty needed for this was miles distant from fancy and illusion, and, on the other hand, it was decidedly susceptible to insensible reality in the manner of the Greek *poietes.* The prose is unprosaically pregnant with meter; many of his paragraphs can be written in verse form. In 1906, in the issue for February 17, he replies to a man who wanted shorter paragraphs: "My trouble is that I never can really feel that there is such a thing as a different subject. There is no such thing as an irrelevant thing in the universe; for all things in the universe are at least relevant to the universe."

The combination of introspection and extroversion had to conclude, as it always has, in delusion or Catholicism; as he predicted in his *William Blake* a dozen years before his own conversion, "If every human being lived a thousand years, every human being would end up either in utter pessimistic skepticism or in the Catholic creed." All his weekly articles, and of course his books, were paving stones in his road to

Rome, which finally received him in 1922. If they seem to speak of everything but religion, it was because he had decided from their start that there can be nothing but religion. He concocted his own *Summa* in his book on St. Francis, where appears his conclusion that if men do not convert, it is because they are not catholic enough to be Catholic. Hidden dogmas and high apologetic jut in and out of his sentences with casualness born of a long tradition, for Christ was his own peripatetic school, tossing chunks of heaven to those who with him walked the broadlit Galilean paths. By a derivative equation, Chesterton wrote wherever he could, in trains and taverns, often dictating in a rush as the infernal deadline neared.

> But I, whose copy is extremely late
> And ought to have been sent an hour before
> I still sit here and trifle with my fate
> And idly write another ballad more.
> I know it is too late; all is o'er,
> And all my writings they will now refuse
> I shall be sacked next Monday. So be sure
> And read the *Illustrated London News.*

And the procrastination continues, but as the ruminations of an unseen labor; to the contradiction of Horace's epigram, when this mountain finally gave birth, another mountain was born. His diction is loud, as befits one who loved the very sight of Fleet Street and who hymned to "the great lights burning on through darkness to dawn and the roar of the printing wheels". The Ciceronianisms of Newman were attributed to his habit of playing a violin before composition; Chesterton seems to have tuned up on a bugle. On a bugle, that is, and a set of chimes; for there is a crystalline cut in every declaration such as intimidates the modern essayist accustomed to muddy sentences flaccid with subjunctives. The situation cannot improve soon when today's minds are not adept at either strings or horn, and passive modernity's chief instrument is the stereo amplifier.

For all his self-mockery about journalism being inherently

bad literature, to dismiss the media out of hand would be to dismiss the great man himself: "It was not the superficial or silly or jolly part of me that made me a journalist. On the contrary, it is such part as I have in what is serious or even solemn."[5] He means of course real solemnity and not the perennial substitute for it, which is pomposity. Let us recall the important warning about this made by the hapless Vice President Spiro Agnew, when he struck a chord in the populist heart by saying Eric Sevareid announced the evening news as though he were reciting Solemn High Mass. As a portentous kind of paraliturgy, the style still obtains; the broadcast media tend even to boast about their own high priesthood, claiming to intercede for the people, when in fact the people are launching an anticlerical rebellion. Most public indicators place popular confidence in the media almost as low as the common esteem for Congress. Certainly media executives are more likely to speak to the people rather than for them. According to reliable surveys, less than 12 percent of these executives believe in God, 85 percent condone adultery and homosexuality, and over 90 percent consider themselves liberal Democrats. It is hardly representative of the population, and it is far removed from what E. C. Bentley described as Chesterton's definition of journalism, "being engaged in direct democratic appeal to the reading public".

If I sound like a false Pharisee, I protest that I may be a genuine Pharisee. And so I allow myself to be scandalized where scandal is due. Chesterton did it in his finer way many times. For instance, his delicate criticisms of America are far removed from those of his beloved Dickens. But he did get his points across ever so diplomatically. On his first trip to America, he announced he would not travel farther west than Chicago, because having seen it, after having seen Jerusalem, he had seen the two extremes of civilization. And we are well familiar with his comment on the electric billboard displays along Broadway,

[5] G. K. Chesterton, *The Autobiography of G. K. Chesterton* (New York: Sheed and Ward, 1936), 289.

that this would make a "glorious garden of wonders" for "anyone who was lucky enough to be unable to read".[6] Today he might say the same of *The Washington Post.* I think he would also be aware of the room for improvement in much of the church press, which lacks only the innocence, while retaining the naïveté, of the style satirized by Flannery O'Connor. The graver problem now is that, at the moment the Catholic social vision is the one cohesive and systematic guide to repairing the classical social contract, some Catholic journalists still are trapped in a Kennedy-Camelot time warp, bewildered by the realities of the present social revolution.

> The whole modern Press, has a perpetual and consuming terror of plain morals. Men always attempt to avoid condemning a thing upon merely moral grounds. If I beat my grandmother to death to-morrow in the middle of Battersea Park, you may be perfectly certain that people will say everything about it except the simple and fairly obvious fact that it is wrong. . . . But of this simple moral explanation modern journalism has, as I say, a standing fear. It will call the action anything else—mad, bestial, vulgar, idiotic, rather than call it sinful.[7]

As it did then, so does it scream true now: though in a society with more judges on more benches than ever, and more critics of more arts and sciences than the world has ever known, it is all the madder to avoid mentioning sin on the grounds that to do so is judgmental. And this at least in part is because the media, which I take to mean journalism and the broadcast industry as a general referent, have commonly questioned any governing moral imperative save selfishness. They even want the legitimate judges in the courts to be nonjudgmental; nor should teachers or preachers or parents make judgments, for all

[6] G. K. Chesterton, *The End of the Armistice* (New York: Sheed and Ward, 1936), 216.

[7] G. K. Chesterton, *All Things Considered* (New York: Sheed and Ward, 1956), 110–11.

judging is willful and fatuous unless, say the media, the media are the judges. So their chief ceremonies are judging and awarding those who during the course of each year in their industry have shown the least judgment. The King James Version says with effective diction of Zaccheus: "And he sought to see Jesus who he was; and could not for the press" (Lk 19:3).

So Chesterton held before the public a truth, and he flaunted it with a glee that is still before us, perhaps more poignantly so now than then: the enemy of ideas is not dogma but ideology. Now ideology is the secular equivalent of liberalism in religion, imputing integrity to a thought just because the self has thought it. Media humbug is rooted in the substitution of ideology for theology. It seeks influence instead of truth. The ideologue imposes a monopoly on mental industry. For all his arrogation of the prophetic mantle, he will not jeopardize his social perquisites for the sake of the social good. A daily case, and a loud one, is that of the writer who thinks of himself as a bold humanitarian yet who does not dare to criticize the conspicuously malignant effect of rock music because its popularity has enormous financial and political power. With less cause, though with courage, Chesterton in *Avowals and Denials* said of jazz what anyone with a fully developed brain stem should say of the sociopathic form of sound known as hard rock: that it is the "very reverse of liberty", for it is "the expression of the pessimistic idea that nature never gets beyond nature", and so "it is the song of the treadmill."

I have mentioned the influence Chesterton had on the father of communications theory, Marshall McLuhan, through *What's Wrong with the World;* it is right, I think, to locate many of the media's faults in a general refusal to trace what is wrong with the world to evil. The secular notion of disorder, of which religious liberalism is just a cultic expression, is at heart tragic, prescinding from systematic thought, estimating moral disintegration to be an inescapable consequence of absurdity. Étienne Gilson held that there is "no necessary connection between philosophical dogmatism and political tyranny, no more than between philosophical skepticism and political liberty". And why? Because, as he said in words almost verbatim Chesterton, "only those who hold something as true are in a position to be tolerant; sceptics cannot be tolerant, only permissive." You cannot adequately assess the demoralization of the media without allowing this important distinction, for what the media tend to call permissiveness is anything but tolerance; they refuse to tolerate the substantial indications of the natural virtues which reject such permissiveness. The media are intolerant of modesty.

The believing Chesterton spoke of sin and forgivable sinners; his permissive opponents denied sin, and, when it served the purposes of their ideology, they gave no quarter to anyone who sinned nonetheless. The press may romanticize promiscuity and at the same time act scandalized when a public figure they do not like is caught in adultery; more than once such a figure has had to quit his career because those who deny that adultery is sinful have refused to forgive his adultery. It is the opposite of the Christian method. The secular mind is incapable of judgment because it is full of scandal; and apparently no one is more easily scandalized than the libertine. The libertine is obliged to humanize his social default by affecting the forms of civilization, but this merely renders dignity pompous and makes morality legalistic. This mentality needs its own shrines and rituals, but, like any esoteric cult, these stand empty and faintly ridiculous. The rationalists were serious when they placed the heart of Voltaire in the Pantheon; there are liberal sentimentalists today who would as reverently enshrine the brain of Jane Fonda. Chesterton represents the rare soul capable of enjoying the spectacle. By cultivating humility instead of a sense of superiority, he avoided condescension in his indulgence of the human comedy. He suffered fools gladly, even deliciously, because his one target was the cant that makes the grand comedy a farce.

The ideologue's commentary occupies the airwaves and newspapers with a bias he would not permit in anyone else; indeed the ideologue insists that the most informed and helpful prejudices of the wise are contemptible biases, while his own rampant biases are valiant convictions. Here is the cause of the ideologue's incapacity for friendly debate; as there is no truth but only convenience, opposite opinion is nothing but opposition. In his autobiography, Chesterton already lamented the intellectual friendships of the Victorian Age, when "a glow of convivial courtesy covered everything; and the wine of friendship could never moult a feather." A photograph of him at adult play with Bernard Shaw and H. G. Wells all dressed in cowboy suits is a fading memento of that wild amity. It is not so today. He could speak of friends "who never differed except in opinion". He could not speak so paradoxically now. And he would be sadly perplexed to meet the classes of people who no longer engage in debate, who do not volunteer direct answers to direct questions, who fall silent when asked their opinion and grumble later among the like-minded. This lack of simple nobility is the most defaming characteristic of false charity, the pretense to honest reserve by which mediocrity conducts itself when it substitutes ambition for ability. Once it was confined to the Trollopian world of careerist clerics and minor politicians; it has become the genre of the age. And when proved wrong by the facts of life and the tide of events, the creature of the age is not deterred nor is he ashamed; to be wrong is not to the ideologue what it is to the sage. The ideologue takes wrong to mean weak, and if he can place himself in a more advantageous position, he will think himself vindicated, though every prophet and commandment point against him. If his argument is false, he grabs it more tightly in a suffocating attempt to strengthen it; and if he is caught in a lie, he shouts it all the more to make it a tocsin of truth.

On Putting Things into Shape

Lacking real humanism, any broadcast medium becomes the message, not in the Christian sense of incarnating truth but in the Gnostic sense of substituting impressions for truth. Gnosticism elevates perception to the level of fact; it makes the medium a religion. Judaeo-Christian culture communicates, by book and speech, truth as it has been historically experienced. The epistemological heresy of Islam was to exaggerate this by literalizing revelation as words in a book rather than as the Living Word. The role of the Quran is different from that of the Bible. Christian fundamentalism is, methodologically, more Islamic than Judaeo-Christian. But Jews and Christians and Muslims all require literacy, while the spirit of Gnosticism is illiterate. And as illiteracy spreads, culture ripens for Gnosticism. The more superficial our culture becomes, the more deracinated it becomes from its own patrimony, and the more it seeks direction from sensory illusions and trivialities. To take just one case, how else can we explain the annual lists of the world's most admired people, consisting merely of the best-known people, with Mother Teresa sandwiched between Elizabeth Taylor and Joan Collins? There is an aura of unreality about it, and television excites the confusion of fact and impression. A woman told me that, having watched me twice on a video tape, she thought I seemed more relaxed the second time. A normal person might detect in this a guileless pathology. Without a transcendent locus, the electronic medium threatens to make the viewer part of the machine. And the television generation actually does begin to speak as a machine: instead of saying "I love it" and "I hate it", there are those who are beginning to say "It turns me on" and "It turns me off."

The media have not conspicuously elevated the quality of critical thought. Professional advertisers now as a policy direct the scripts to the comprehension level of a fourteen-year-old, as that has become the norm of American perception. This is not promising. The author of *Mein Kampf* attributed the beginning of his success to his decision to appeal to this same mental age. And, needless to say, the thirty-second campaign advertisement on television discourages deeper analysis; even debates have been replaced by a succession of "sound bites" and the thrill of shouting. That any of what we have come to call presidential debates could be considered real debates would have been laughable to the audiences of Shaw and Chesterton and Belloc in the Albert Hall.

Images and Idols

The symbol, important as it is, becomes a menace when it replaces fact. But a culture will allow that to happen if it does not think there really are facts. All is impression. If the media respect the life of the mind, why are there so few bald news commentators? Chesterton was the rare figure of a man with lots of hair and lots of brains, but any producer today would tell him he had a weight problem. Lincoln would never have been allowed on the screen. If the intention of media gnosis is to convey only an image, it creates electronic idolatry. The Psalmist spoke almost as a censor of icy politicians whose images are created and molded by the media and whose ideas are shaped by those agents who are rather dreadfully known as their handlers: "They have mouths, but do not speak; eyes but do not see. They have ears, but do not hear; noses but do not smell. They have hands but do not feel; feet but do not walk; and they do not make a sound in their throat. Those who make them are like them; so are all who trust in them" (Ps 115:5–8). Chesterton's political maturation peaked the day he realized how the press carves these idols. He had heard a tedious and almost incomprehensible speech from a meek man in a Liberal club, and the next day read the headline in the Cadbury press: "Lord Spencer Unfurls Banner."

Comparisons are odious, but Chesterton was on the way to becoming a little like pre-Roosevelt Democrats, or roughly what more recently were called Reagan Democrats. Elite populists mocked them when they were called the Silent Majority, but Chesterton had discerned the species more than a generation earlier:

Smile at us, pay us, pass us; but do not quite forget;
For we are the people of England, that never have spoken
    yet...
We hear men speaking for us of new laws strong and
    sweet,
Yet is there no man speaketh as we speak in the street.
It may be we shall rise the last as Frenchmen rose the first,
Our wrath come after Russia's wrath and our wrath be
    the worst.
It may be we are meant to mark with our riot and our
    rest
God's scorn for all men governing. It may be beer is best.
But we are the people of England, and we have not spoken
    yet.[8]

By 1910, Chesterton, whose own commitments had been to the Liberal party, had decided that Liberalism was the "L" word, and his reasons are not without present analogy. At the time of the accession of King George V, the suburban voters and urban middle class were drifting away from Liberalism, while the poor were losing patience with it, giving it some tenuous allegiance but scouting alternatives, mainly Labour. The Liberal victory of 1910, like the election of Lyndon Johnson, was Pyrrhic; for it positioned the party to preside over the social fragmentation caused by a war. It ruined the party; the chief support remaining for Liberalism was from the media establishment who claimed to speak for the man in the street because they had just run him over. Their case matches what Ronald Knox remarked of the Oxford Union when it voted the resolution not to serve King and Country in the event of another war: having turned their backs on the nation, they had the effrontery to say that they had the nation behind them.

In the heyday of Fabian Socialism, the Liberal party lined up behind Lloyd George, whose definition of reality did not exhaust

---

[8] *The Collected Poems of G. K. Chesterton* (London: Cecil Palmer, 1927), 157–60.

facts; and Winston Churchill, who did acknowledge facts and changed parties, inherited the condemnation of the press as a traitor, as later would Mr. Reagan and Mrs. Kirkpatrick. Chesterton would find their motives plausible. His objection was to that unsteady humanitarianism that cannot define what is human. He complained that the social-engineering philanthropist is not a brother; he is a supercilious aunt.

So the prophetic man measured disorder and order alike in this malignant philanthropy by a scale that involved God and Satan. In *Orthodoxy,* he says reform means "we see a certain thing out of shape and we mean to put it into shape. And we know what shape." Secularism did not know the shape. It had gotten the world wrong by committing the unnatural act of measuring nature apart from the immanent standards of good and evil. And in this lies the secret of Chesterton's towering humility: what he wrote about nature was not his own, but rather his own way of putting it. The "it" was the original shape of reality. This seemed novel, and even unfit for modern thought, because the people encountering this oldest thing in the world were new. Chesterton did not plagiarize in the despicable and low sense; his was an inspired plagiarism that forsakes incidental sources for the Source. It pillages the treasury of the saints. Such heavenly theft marks the genius from the hack. The procedure was according to high dogma, blushing though the pallor of civil events which are the incidental subjects of his journalistic essays. It makes each of his columns in *The Illustrated London News,* for instance, a flickering votive light to the orthodox creeds. I cannot imagine Schopenhauer getting his ideas through elegies to local cheeses, the shape of men's noses, snails and *The Mikado.* But this is precisely what Chesterton did to reach the truth each week. He was a foremost example of Quintillian's *vir bonus docendi peritus:* the good man who speaks from practical knowledge. And he was not content to pass on interesting bits of information as isolated items; as surely as the whole Mediterranean had once washed well within the circumference of Virgil's fine skull, and the Brooklyn Bridge spanned the lobes of Roebling's brain, the whole experience of Christian humanism cavorted in the head of Chesterton at his weekly dictation.

Media Metaphysics

At our critical juncture, as at his, there is much poignantly ignorant soul-searching about what philosophical foundation is needed for a true commonweal. A woman once told Maisie Ward that she had long found Chesterton's politics peculiar because she had been "brought up to think that it was quite right for the poor to have their teeth brushed by officials".[9] Chesterton was nearly unique among journalists in bringing this down to very clear metaphysics and anthropology, without using the terms. He writes in 1926: "The critic of the State can only exist where a religious sense of right protects his claim to his own bow and spear; or at least, to his own pen or his own printing press."[10]

If the bywords and asides in his essays expose one deceit more than any other, it is the modern refusal to acknowledge its surrender to the tyranny of the cliché. He did not live to see the pusillanimity of the academic establishment in the face of campus radicalism in the 1960s and 1970s, but he studied its seedling in the meeting halls of the vegetarian Socialists. Those statist utopians wanted to eliminate illiteracy by means of philosophical vagaries which, by undermining confidence in objective truth, have quite effectively dismantled literacy and logic by now. This was not by neglect or default, nor was it unravelled by unwieldy forces. It was crusaded and campaigned for as staunchly as earlier literate reforms. The banalities of modern progressivism abound, and if their causes are ignored and if

[9] Ward, 296.
[10] See Alzina Stone Dale, *The Outline of Sanity* (Grand Rapids: Eerdmans, 1982), 185.

they are promoted by the media as logical and wise, their consequences are inescapable nonetheless. By the 1920s, Chesterton was predicting: "The next great heresy is going to be simply an attack on morality, and especially on sexual morality. The madness of tomorrow is not in Moscow, but much more in Manhattan." We are living in that tomorrow. New York City, for example, has consecutively legalized sodomy and criminalized smoking in public places; at the end of the twentieth century, unnatural carnal union is an indictable offense only if it is done while smoking a cigar. This would have been a parable for Chesterton in the first decade of the century; in the last decade it is a current event. His pen would have run wild if the media of his day had supported abortion while courting hysteria over the plight of three beached whales in Alaska. He would have rallied terrible words if he had read the British medical journal *The Lancet,* which in August of 1994, while defending abortion, recommended the use of pain killers for the foetus in late-term abortions, especially those involving dismemberment.

In the lush Edwardian parade of life, one would not have expected that the chief moral questions at the end of the century would involve infanticide and the definition of motherhood, or that theological faculties would include self-proclaimed witches, or that the chief social fear would be about plague. But week by week, on trams or in his little study, a conspicuous character with furrowed brow and shocks of trembling hair was diagramming how it all could happen. The intellectually honest response now is to reexamine what he wrote; in the universities he still is avoided, and those of intellectual pretensions who ignore him continue their limp submission to mediocrity, awarding each other meaningless degrees and wondering why the world does not take them altogether seriously. The only ones left who read Chesterton are the meanest men who keep being immortal. And, in a curious way, the one who points this out will find himself dismissed as an obscurantist and an elitist; in fact, such a one only has a democratic appetite for excellence, and that appetite is not highly developed by modern trendiness and insecurity.

But Chesterton would also have certainly said that neoconservatism, when it is innocent of a true metaphysic, is feckless in current battles of logic and is as deluded as Fabian optimism and as depressing as modern deconstructionism. He wrote when barely twenty-eight years old:

> We live in the Tory revival. That is to say, we live in a world in which artists care for nothing but art, and ethicalists for nothing but ethics. . . . There was a time when art and morals together were part of a great general view of life called philosophy or religion. . . . But in the great breakdown of belief which is the beginning of the new Toryism, they have, for a sign, been totally separated. Law has become cruel in Henley and art supercilious in Whistler—both because they have been separated from the rest of life. Men have become idolatrous towards these things and treated art and morality respectively as gods. For assuredly they are children of God and when God has been eliminated, they may be called, for want of anything better, his heirs. As they look to us today with their melancholy eyes, they may be heirs; they are certainly orphans.[11]

On the whole, Chesterton's columns are happy essays; each goes up like a flare in the night, and for a moment signs of life are visible on the ground. But only for a moment. Our new system of education, which has by now formed a generation of media executives, has produced a servile mentality that is not habituated to acute analysis, and the flares from Chesterton's pen may appear as sparks and not beacons. Chesterton expected more of the public than do our current newspaper and television industries. A university president at a recent commencement benignly raised his robed arms over the graduates in a Mosaic gesture and, to my surprise, dismissed them with an

[11] *The Daily News,* March 18, 1911.

un-Mosaic burp: "May you find satisfaction." No longer would the end of human endeavor be happiness, the scholastic mark of freedom and the true trophy after a length of Socratic discontent. Now it would be satiety, and I could see row upon row of young upwardly mobile professionals marching out into the world to stuff themselves. It is probably a formula for unhappiness; it is certainly a formula for slavery. The placid nihilism of our generation is the deadliest land mine laid by the departing modernists.

I would hope, not in a spirit of recrimination but as a scientific kind of historical duty, that a future generation will label the various ruins of our age with the names of the movements and movers who wrecked them: that each denuded church sanctuary resembling a cocktail lounge would bear the name of the renovator who whitewashed the florid faces of the saints, that each ugly commercial building would advertise the architect who relocated human life to fester in it, that the epitaph of each victim of vice might name the sirens who sang a sexual revolution, that each asylum be named for each psychoanalyst who said there is no sin. I propose it only as a guide away from the intolerable cruelty of unreality. Chesterton proposed something like it himself in an encounter with the lady who announced that the craving to do a thing shows you ought to do it. As the train in which they were travelling rolled on and the insanity flitted away, he saw the moral carnage of such flippancy on the passing fields of England and the world:

> Madam, you will not, I am sure be anything but delighted to learn that you have convinced me. A man should always do a thing as long as he has a genuine craving to do it. How true that is! How illuminating! And yet how simple! My present genuine craving, which is to strike you suddenly and sharply on the bridge of the nose, is one which as it is far less destructive than meat-eating, will certainly command your theoretical acquiescence, and which also has this advantage, that it will give some sort of glimmering notion of what sort of world you are living in. As you say, I may survive the craving.

After beating you on the nose for a day or two the desire itself may leave me. Then, no doubt, I shall pass to a higher plane.[12]

It remains to be seen whether natural virtue and its respect for natural law can withstand the general media onslaught against them. Time will tell if the common man can keep common sense: "Materialism says the universe is mindless; and faith says it is ruled by the highest mind. Neither will be satisfied with the new progressive creed, which declares hopefully that the universe is half-witted."[13] Chesterton read ominous portents in the way the press treated subjects from the suffragette movement to art and the theater. There was a growth in cults and spiritualism after the First World War, and the fantastic theosophists included not only gurus imported from the East but trendy fixtures of the religious establishment like Dean Inge of St. Paul's Cathedral, dear to the media's attention. Some of Inge's own columns on the Catholic modernists had the same sniffy "plague on both your houses" attitude that complects the iconoclastic religion editors of some of our major newspapers. In 1905, Chesterton had called iconoclasm "the lowest of all the unskilled trades".[14] And his words on the death of Pius X might be redirected to those pundits who have criticized in life a Polish successor to that Pontiff:

As has been pointed out, with subtle power and all proper delicacy, in numberless liberal and large-minded journals, the great and good priest now dead had all the prejudices of a peasant. He had a prejudice to the effect that the mystical word "Yes" should be distinguished from the equally unfathomable expression "No".... But there was something more in him that would not have been in the ordinary peasant. For all this time he had wept for our tears; and he broke his heart for our bloodshed.[15]

[12] *The Illustrated London News,* April 28, 1906.
[13] G. K. Chesterton, *The Uses of Diversity* (London: Library Press, 1920), 170.
[14] *The Daily News,* April 26, 1905.
[15] *The Illustrated London News,* August 29, 1914.

In his own English way, this is also what Chesterton did. And his sternest criticism of the modern media, whose germ he knew and whose good potential he never discounted, was its failure to weep and break its heart. Those who "talk grossly about a sensitive and austere topic" represent the "stunted mind and an idiot lightheartedness, which is altogether peculiar to our civilization."[16] On the occasion of a recent airplane crash, a television reporter asked a ten-year-old girl what she thought about the death of her mother. The moral atrophy is different only in transparency, but not in degree, from the general ineptness of commentators in evaluating the facts of culture. Society is burdened with social critics who boast little awareness of the artifacts of civilization, whose word processors are bloodless and who do not feel the pulse of whole ages. These are the vulgarians whose defacements, according to Chesterton, are worse than the defacements of mere barbarians. The tendency of contemporary editorialization is toward that morally bankrupt secularism which is a way of being of the world while hardly in it; it may be so because journalists of limited prudence are susceptible to the fatuousness of intellectual trends in whose derivative light they would bask. The Fabian Socialists tweaked by Chesterton were playfully gamboling creatures compared to the lumbering dinosaurs of progressivism who now bellow on the edge of their own extinction. The occluded visionaries of theological modernism promised to soar through the Edwardian sky; at the end of the century, they are plummeting with twisted talons already half-fossilized. Chesterton spent his life affirming what the modernizer denied, the axiom on which all the modern axes have been blunted: he said that the meanest man is immortal, but the mightiest movement is temporal.

[16] *G. K.'s Weekly,* January 1, 1927.

Large as Life

Too often has Chesterton been called larger than life. He can only be that to those who are smaller than life. He was not larger than life, for then he would not have been alive. Chesterton was precisely as large as life, and he was one of the few who know how large that is. So, his journalism was historic, and he lamented how journalism had come to replace history: "There exists in the modern world, perhaps for the first time in history, a class of people whose interest is not that things should happen well or happen badly, should happen successfully or happen unsuccessfully, should happen to the advantage of this party or the advantage of that party, but whose interest simply is that things should happen."[17]

One of the most compelling and benignly eccentric figures I have known was a Church of England vicar, Philip Bayard Clayton, known as "Tubby" by his curate, by George VI and everyone else, I think. He had been Warden of the Tower of London and so distinguished himself in the First World War that the Belgian government put his face on a postage stamp. On one trip in the late 1960s, we spent days walking through seemingly endless military cemeteries in Flanders as he recounted battles from Crecy to Verdun. At each stop he required recitation of Laurence Binyon's poem. Only recently did I discover an article in a 1927 issue of *G.K.'s Weekly* in which Chesterton mentions that he and Tubby had been schoolfellows. And there he quotes the same poem we said at the graves:

> They shall grow not old, as we that are left grow old:
> Age shall not weary them, nor the years condemn.
> At the going down of the sun and in the morning
> We will remember them.

[17] G. K. Chesterton: *The Ball and the Cross* (New York: John Lane, 1910), 68.

There were giants in the pocked land in those days. Something more than we can account for produced such characters not larger than life but in the full measure of life fully lived. The media are obliged to report the true scale of living in fact beyond miniature or caricature. It cannot be done by a journalism that is "the most shapeless, careless, and colourless work done in our day".[18] If there were giants in the land then, there can be giants now. It is, after all, the same land, and we are of the same human stock, and the times and issues are certainly no less important. A small-minded journalist or broadcaster may think giants are freaks, and he may want to bring them down, even as he is trying to inflate really small people who are his idea of big people. Such was not the method of G. K. Chesterton. So as he lay dying in his Beaconsfield house, the Dominican friar Vincent McNabb sang the "Salve Regina" and kissed the pen on the bedside table. If Chesterton late of Fleet Street is now able to intercede for the media, there may come a regeneration when we shall kiss some of their word processors and television screens.

As his writings are recovered from the attics where advocates of free speech locked him, new ideologues continue to shun Chesterton. When that fails, they patronize his "clever" style and change the subject. "Those who detest the harmless writer of this column are generally reduced (in their final ecstasy of anger) to calling him brilliant; which has long ago in our journalism become a mere expression of contempt."[19] But that cannot be done with impunity, for Chesterton is not the subject; the subject is the Changeless, and how we are changed by Him whenever the soul catches a flash of His light. Like the children he described, Chesterton resembled the Thomist God living "in an almost timeless world".[20] And exactly because of that, his words have the impact of immediacy when most newspaper essays and television commentaries are devoured by anachronisms.

It can only be because the first evangelists were journalists, and any great journalist must likewise be evangelistic if he is not to be an ideologue: loving to write, but also knowing the content of the love which impels the writing. It will be so, not by reporting the great creeds and dogmas of life, for that is not the proper enterprise of the secular media, but by chronicling the daily calls cried by pedlars and prime ministers as part of a spherical music, more mysterious than the chants of the whales swimming the sea and the radio waves bounced off a far mercurial planet, and enchanting as the harmony Lorenzo rhymed of in *The Merchant of Venice,* "still quiring to the young-eyed cherubins".

G. K. Chesterton flung out words as lyrics to the universal, and they remain to be sung even when the world seems close to forgetting the tune. The searing logic of his slapdash lines can seem so byzantine to us in "this muddy vesture of decay" that they may be best understood by that most arcane of intellects, whose laureate he hoped to attain after a lifetime of getting the message across: the rare and dread species of thinker known as the amateur. And if a thinker thinks as deeply as a real amateur should, he will discover that an amateur is a lover; and if the lover loves as deeply as a lover should, he may become one of those saints God raises up in critical times to see the times through the crisis.

INDEX OF PROPER NAMES

197